TALK TO ME IN KOREAN
LEVEL 4

Learn to Compare, Contrast,
Modify, and Describe More Fluently
in Korean!

This book is based on a series of published lessons, divided into ten levels, which are currently available at https://talktomeinkorean.com.

Talk To Me In Korean - Level 4

1판 1쇄 • 1st edition published	2016. 5. 16.	
1판 15쇄 • 15th edition published	2024. 9. 2.	
지은이 • Written by	Talk To Me In Korean	
책임편집 • Edited by	선경화 Kyung-hwa Sun, 스테파니 베이츠 Stephanie Bates	
디자인 • Designed by	선윤아 Yoona Sun	
삽화 • Illustrations by	김경해 Kyounghae Kim	
녹음 • Voice Recordings by	선현우 Hyunwoo Sun, 최경은 Kyeong-eun Choi, 석다혜 Dahye Seok, 선경화 Kyung-hwa Sun	
펴낸곳 • Published by	롱테일북스 Longtail Books	
펴낸이 • Publisher	이수영 Su Young Lee	
편집 • Copy-edited by	김보경 Florence Kim	
주소 • Address	04033 서울특별시 마포구 양화로 113, 3층(서교동, 순흥빌딩)	
	3rd Floor, 113 Yanghwa-ro, Mapo-gu, Seoul, KOREA	
이메일 • E-mail	TTMIK@longtailbooks.co.kr	
ISBN	979-11-86701-36-2 14710	

TTMIK - TALK TO ME IN KOREAN

MESSAGE
FROM
THE AUTHOR

Welcome to Level 4. Can you believe that you have made it to the 4th level already? Congratulations!

You are about to take a giant leap forward in understanding and speaking Korean. After studying with this book, you will be more comfortable with making your own Korean sentences, have a broader Korean vocabulary, and be more familiar with reading only 한글 (Han-geul) rather than relying on romanization.

To help you become more accustomed to reading only 한글, no romanization will be provided from Level 4 onward. If you feel that you read a bit slower without the romanization, please do not worry or become too frustrated. Over time and with practice, you WILL become comfortable with reading 한글 and you will find yourself reading and comprehending much faster without romanization. It may seem impossible right now, but we know you can do it!

There are a lot of exciting and useful lessons waiting for you in the future, so we hope you continue to study with us. We appreciate each and every one of you who have decided to join us on your journey to learning Korean, and we promise to bring you only the best and most useful Korean learning material. 여러분 정말 감사합니다!

TABLE OF CONTENTS

LESSON 1

The more..., the more...

-(으)면 -(으)ㄹ수록

Track 01

For the first lesson in Level 4, you will learn how to say "the more [A], the more [B]" in Korean.

"The more [A]" is expressed through the verb ending -(으)ㄹ수록, and the latter "the more [B]" part is expressed through another verb.

> ### *Conjugation*
>
> - Verb stems ending with a consonant + -을수록
> - Verb stems ending with a vowel + -ㄹ수록
> - (Exception) Verb stems ending with ㄹ + -수록

Ex)

살다 → 살수록 = the more you live, the more...

가다 → 갈수록 = the more you go, the more...

예쁘다 → 예쁠수록 = the prettier it is, the more...

8

비싸다 → 비쌀수록 = the more expensive it is, the more ...

이상하다 → 이상할수록 = the stranger it is, the more ...

바쁘다 → 바쁠수록 = the busier you are, the more ...

Usages

1. 맛있다 = 맛있 + -을수록 = 맛있을수록

Ex)
맛있을수록 잘 팔려요.

= The more delicious it is, the better it sells.

2. 바쁘다 = 바쁘 + -ㄹ수록 = 바쁠수록

Track 01

Ex)
바쁠수록 건강이 중요해요.

= The busier you are, the more important your health is.

3. 사람이 많다 = 사람이 많 + -을수록 = 사람이 많을수록

Ex)
사람이 많을수록 좋아요.

= The more people, the better.

* Note
Although -(으)ㄹ수록 basically translates to "the more [A], the more [B]", the meaning can change depending on the context of the conversation. -(으)ㄹ수록 can also express the

9

meaning of:

(1) "Even more so, especially when…"

(2) "Especially if…" or "even more…"

(3) "Particularly when…"

Ex)

바쁠수록 잠을 많이 자야 돼요.

= (lit.) The busier you are, the more you need to sleep.

= You need to sleep more, particularly when you are busy.

학생일수록 책을 많이 읽어야 돼요.

= You need to read a lot of books, even more so if you are a student.

Track 01

Using -(으)ㄹ수록 with -(으)면

Using -(으)ㄹ수록 on its own is already enough, but sometimes the speaker wants to emphasize his/her point a little better. This can be achieved by using the same verb stem that would be used with -(으)ㄹ수록 and attaching it to -(으)면.

바쁠수록 = 바쁘면 바쁠수록
좋을수록 = 좋으면 좋을수록

Ex)

The more, the better.

= 많을수록 좋아요.

= 많으면 많을수록 좋아요.

Learn to Compare, Contrast, Modify,

The cheaper it is, the more of it you can buy.

= 쌀수록 많이 살 수 있어요.

= 싸면 쌀수록 많이 살 수 있어요.

Set expression

The expression "갈수록" comes from 가다 + -(으)ㄹ수록 and literally means "the more you go". However, it is used as more of a set expression which means "more and more so in time" or "as time goes by".

갈수록 추워요.

= It keeps getting colder.

Track 01

사브린 씨는 갈수록 한국어를 잘해요.

= Sabrin keeps getting better at Korean.

Sample Sentences

친구는 많을수록 좋아요.

= (When it comes to friends,) The more friends you have, the better.

= 친구는 많으면 많을수록 좋아요.

비쌀수록 잘 팔려요.

= The more expensive it is, the better it sells.

= 비싸면 비쌀수록 잘 팔려요.

11

재미있는 사람일수록 좋아요.

= The more interesting a person is, the better.

재미있는 사람일수록 인기가 많아요.

= The more interesting a person is, the more popular he/she is.

= If you are an interesting person, it is more likely that you are popular.

Track 01

Learn to Compare, Contrast, Modify,

Sample Dialogue

Track
02

A: 언제까지 결정해야 돼요?

B: 빠르면 빠를수록 좋아요.

A: 그럼 빨리 결정해서 알려 줄게요.

A: *When do I have to make a decision by?*

B: *The earlier, the better.*

A: *Alright, I will decide soon and let you know.*

13

✏ Exercises for Lesson 1

Match the following Korean words with the appropriate conjugation:

1. 살다 (= to live)

        a. -을수록

2. 가다 (= to go)

3. 맛있다 (= to be tasty)

        b. -ㄹ수록

4. 생각하다 (= to think)

        c. -수록

5. 밀다 (= to push)

Check the answers on **p.188**

Learn to Compare, Contrast, Modify,

LESSON **2**

Do you want to...?

-(으)ㄹ래요?

If you have studied with Talk To Me In Korean until this point, you are already familiar with the future tense verb ending -(으)ㄹ 거예요. Do you remember how to use it? In case it has slipped your mind, here's a quick refresher:

Track
03

-(으)ㄹ 거예요 can be used to express plain future tense sentences.

> **Ex)**
> 내일 갈 거예요. = I am going to go tomorrow.

Now that it is starting to come back to you, take the opportunity to build upon that knowledge and continue this lesson on -(으)ㄹ래요.

Meaning

-(으)ㄹ래요 is used when expressing the intent or the will to do something. If you place a question mark at the end of the sentence, you can ask about someone else's will or intention

15

to do something, such as in "Do you want to...?" When used as a statement, it can mean "I want to..." or "I am going to...".

Conjugation

Verb stems ending with a consonant + -을래요
Ex) 먹다 (to eat) becomes 먹을래요.

Verb stems ending with the consonant ㄹ + -래요
Ex) 팔다 (to sell) becomes 팔래요.

Verb stems ending with a vowel + -ㄹ래요
Ex) 사다 (to buy) becomes 살래요.

Track 03

Sample Sentences

집에 갈래요.

= I want to go home. / I am going to go home.

* Comparison

집에 가고 싶어요. - the most general and vague way

= I want to go home.

집에 갈게요. - looking for feedback / reacting to the situation

= (If so) I will go home. (Implying that you wonder what the other person thinks about it.)

16

집에 갈 거예요. - most direct

= I am going to go home. (Implying that it is your plan to go home.)

혼자 할래요.

= I will do it alone. / I want to do it alone.

   * However, if you say "혼자 할게요" ("I will do it alone (if you do not mind)"), it sounds much nicer.

저는 안 갈래요.

= I do not want to go.

= I am not going to go.

   * "저는 안 가고 싶어요" also means "I do not want to go", but it has some room for change, so it can mean "If you really insist, I might go".

Track 03

뭐 마실래요?

= What do you want to drink?

= What are you going to drink?

   * Although you can ask a person what he/she wants by using the ending "-고 싶어요?" in Korean, it is unnatural and sounds a bit like a textbook. By using the "-(으)ㄹ래요?" ending, you are asking another person what he/she wants to do in such a way that it lets him/her know that he/she is not obligated to answer because of you or in your favor.

커피 마실래요, 차 마실래요?

= Do you want to drink coffee or tea?

17

* This can be very similar to "커피 마시고 싶어요, 차 마시고 싶어요?", but "커피 마실래요, 차 마실래요?" is a more natural way to ask.

이거 볼래?

= Do you want to see this?

언제 만날래?

= When do you want to meet?

* Here, you are talking about "we" or "us", so you can add the word 우리 and say "우리 언제 만날래?" to make the meaning clearer.

Track 03

** Note

The -(으)ㄹ래요 ending is typically used only in casual settings. You cannot use this verb ending if you are talking to someone with whom you must use formal language.

18

Sample Dialogue

Track
04

A: 주소 좀 알려 줄래요?

B: 왜요?

A: 청첩장 보내 줄게요.

A: *Can you let me know your address?*

B: *Why?*

A: *I will send you a wedding invitation card.*

19

✏ Exercises for Lesson 2

a. 집에 갈래요.
b. 집에 갈게요.
c. 집에 갈 거예요.

All the sentences above can be translated to "I am going to go home" in English, but:

1. Which sentence is the most direct way to imply that it is your plan to go home?

( )

2. Which sentence is implying that you wonder what the other person thinks about the fact that you are going to go home?

( )

3. Which one can also be translated to "I want to go home"?

( )

Check the answers on **p.188**

20

LESSON 3

It cannot be...

-(으)ㄹ 리가 없어요

In Korean, when you want to express your disbelief in something that is said, has actually happened, or is happening right at that moment, you can use the ending -(으)ㄹ 리가 없어요.

Track 05

Meaning

-(으)ㄹ 리가 없어요 means "it cannot be..." or "it is impossible that...".

> *Conjugation*
>
> Verb stems ending with a vowel + -ㄹ 리가 없어요.
> Verb stems ending with ㄹ + 리가 없어요.
> Verb stems ending with consonants other than ㄹ + -을 리가 없어요.

Meaning of 리

리 means "reason" or "logic" and can be found in the words "이유 (reason)" and "논리 (logic)".

21

Therefore, the structure -(으)ㄹ 리가 없어요 literally means "there is no reason that..." or "there is no logic behind the fact that...", and when it is translated into English, it means "it cannot be..." or "it is impossible...".

Examples

I. 그렇다 is a very common expression that is used every day in Korean, which means "to be so". When 그렇다 is put together with verb endings, the consonant ㅎ is usually dropped.

그러 + ㄹ 리가 없어요 = 그럴 리가 없어요!

= It cannot be!

= It cannot be so!

= That is impossible!

2. 눈이 오다 = to snow

눈이 오 + ㄹ 리가 없어요 = 눈이 올 리가 없어요!

= It is impossible that it is snowing!

= It cannot be snowing!

3. 모르다 = to not know

모르 + ㄹ 리가 없어요 = 모를 리가 없어요.

= It cannot be that he/she does not know.

= It is impossible that he/she does not know.

Learn to Compare, Contrast, Modify,

Using -(으)ㄹ 리가 없어요 with the past and future tenses

-을 리가 없어요 can be placed after the past tense suffix -았/었/였-. In this case, it is always -을 because the past tense suffixes always end in the consonant ㅆ.

Examples

1. 가다 = to go

[present tense] 가 + -ㄹ 리가 없어요 = 갈 리가 없어요

= There is no way that he/she is going/leaving.

= He/She will never go.

Track 05

[past tense] 가 + -았- + -을 리가 없어요 = 갔을 리가 없어요

= There is no way that he/she went.

2. 있다 = to be (somewhere)

[present tense] 있 + -을 리가 없어요 = 있을 리가 없어요

= There cannot be something.

= There is no way that it exists.

[past tense] 있 + -었- + -을 리가 없어요 = 있었을 리가 없어요

= It is impossible that there was ...

23

For future tense, the same structure as the present tense is used. You can simply add words which indicate that you are talking about a future action or state.

Ex)

내일이 일요일 + -이 + -ㄹ 리가 없어요. = 내일이 일요일일 리가 없어요.

= There is no way that tomorrow is Sunday.

내일 눈이 오 + -ㄹ 리가 없어요. = 내일 눈이 올 리가 없어요.

= It is impossible that it will snow tomorrow.

Sample Sentences

정말요? 그럴 리가 없어요!

= Really? That cannot be true!

효진 씨가 안 왔을 리가 없어요.

= It is impossible that Hyojin did not come.

= There is no way that Hyojin is not here.

경은 씨가 노래를 할 리가 없어요.

= There is no way that Kyeong-eun is going to sing.

= It is impossible that Kyeong-eun will sing.

안 추울 리가 없어요. 지금 1월이에요.

= It is impossible that it is not cold. It is January right now.

이상하네요. 안 될 리가 없어요.

= It is strange. There is no way that it is not going to work.

Sample Dialogue

Track 06

A: 석진 씨 아직 안 왔어요?

B: 네. 전화도 안 받아요.

A: 석진 씨가 늦잠 잘 리가 없는데...

A: Has Seokjin not come yet?

B: No. He's not even answering my phone calls.

A: It can't be that he is oversleeping, though...

✏ *Exercises for Lesson* **3**

Check the answers on **p.188**

1. How do you say "It cannot be that he/she does not know" in Korean?

( )

2. How do you say "It is impossible that it is not cold" in Korean?

( )

3. Translate the following sentence into Korean: "It is impossible that it is not painful".
   * 아프다 = to be painful

( )

4. How do you say "There is no way that he/she went" in Korean?

( )

5. Translate "It is impossible that it will snow tomorrow" to Korean.

( )

26

Learn to Compare, Contrast, Modify,

LESSON 4

Verb Ending: -지(요)

-지(요)

-지(요), just like -네(요)*, is a verb ending which gives Korean sentences a very subtle change in meaning.

Track 07

* Go back to Level 3, Lesson 25 if you need to brush up on the usage of -네(요) and the difference it makes when using it!

Usages

Use -지(요) when:
(I) talking about something, supposing that the other person also already knows about it;
(2) both you and the other person know about something or have a common opinion about something, and you are just mentioning the fact again.

Use -지(요) as an interrogative (question) ending when:
(3) both you and the other person know about something, but you are just reassuring yourself by asking the question;

27

(4) you know about something, and you are asking yourself to confirm the fact. In this case, you do not speak in 존댓말;

(5) you do not know something, so you are asking yourself a question. Usually you are thinking out loud and asking the other people around you at the same time. 반말 is used in this case as well.

Ex)

오늘 금요일이에요. = Today is Friday.

오늘 금요일이네요! = Oh, today is Friday!

오늘 금요일이지요. = Today is Friday.

(You and the other person already know that today is Friday, but you are just confirming out loud that it is, indeed, Friday.)

오늘 금요일이지요? = Today is Friday, right?

(You and the other person already know that today is Friday, but you are just reassuring yourself by asking the question.)

Track 07

Conjugation

Present Tense:

verb stem + -지(요)

Past Tense:

verb stem + -았/었/였- + -지(요)

Future Tense:

verb stem + -(으)ㄹ 거 + -지(요) (almost exclusively used only as an interrogative ending)

Learn to Compare, Contrast, Modify,

Contraction

When speaking in 존댓말, the verb ending -지요 often changes to -죠 for simplicity and ease of pronunciation.

Sample Sentences

오늘 날씨 춥지요?

= The weather is cold today, right?

→ (You know that the other person knows that the weather is cold.)

맞아요. 피자 정말 맛있죠.

= That is right. Pizza really is delicious.

→ (You know that the other person also thinks that pizza is delicious.)

Track 07

재미있지요?

= It is fun, right?

→ (You know that the other person already thinks that it is fun, but you are asking again just to make sure.)

이게 뭐지? (asking oneself)

= What is this?

→ (You are not directly asking anybody, so you do not say "이게 뭐야?" or "이게 뭐예요?")

그럴 수도 있죠.

= Yeah, that could be possible.

→ (You and the other person both know that something is possible, and you are simply expressing your agreement to what the other person is saying.)

29

Sample Dialogue

Track
08

A: 저하고 집에 같이 가요.

B: 네. 기다릴게요.

A: 홍대 쪽으로 가죠?

B: 네.

A: Let's go home together.

B: Okay, I will wait.

A: You are heading toward Hongdae, right?

B: Yes.

Learn to Compare, Contrast, Modify,

✏ Exercises for Lesson 4

Decide if the statement is true or false. If it is false, correct the underlined portion to make the statement true.

Use -지(요) when:

1. talking about something, <u>supposing that the other person also already knows about it.</u>

(   )

2. you and the other person know about something, <u>but have a different opinion about it.</u>

(   )

Use -지(요) as an interrogative (question) ending when:

3. both you and the other person know about something, <u>but you are just reassuring yourself by asking the question.</u>

(   )

4. you know about something, and you are asking yourself to confirm the fact. <u>In this case, you do not speak in 반말.</u>

(   )

5. you do not know something, so you are asking yourself a question. <u>Usually you are talking to yourself quietly so that no one around you can hear it.</u>

(   )

Check the answers on **p.188**

LESSON 5

"당신" and "you"

당신

Track 09

The word 당신 appears in many Korean songs, dramas and movies, but it needs to be used with caution in real-life conversations. Take a closer look at 당신 by following this lesson.

Meaning

In many dictionaries, if you look up the word "you", you will see 당신 as a suitable translation. However, in reality, native Korean speakers rarely use the word "you" in sentences, especially when speaking in 존댓말, or formal language.

당신 may technically mean "you", but the connotation of 당신 is much different than "you" in English. Unless you understand what 당신 means, exactly in what situations you can use it, and how to use it - simply do not use it. Luckily, this lesson is dedicated to helping you understand this pesky, but useful, little word!

32

Well, then when is it that people DO use the word 당신?

You can use the word 당신 when:

1. you are angry at someone and do not mind fighting or arguing with that person;

2. you are translating from a foreign language and you absolutely must have a word for "you";

3. you are writing or singing a song, or are using indirect language in general;

4. you are addressing your spouse (commonly used among middle-aged or older people);

5. (rare case) you are talking about someone (who is not present) in an honorific way and want to say "he" or "she".

Usage 1

당신 뭐야?

= Who do you think you are? / What are you?

당신 뭐가 문제야?

= What is your problem?

Track 09

Using 당신 in this fashion evokes the feeling that you really do not mind getting in a quarrel or a fight with the other person. Note that you are not speaking entirely in 존댓말 anymore. If you are already speaking in 반말, you would say "너".

Usage 2 & 3

당신의 눈은 참 아름다워요.

= Your eyes are so beautiful.

당신에게 이 노래를 바칩니다.

= I dedicate this song to you.

You are forced to use 당신 here because you do not know the name of the other person without context.

Usage 4

당신 지금 어디예요?

= Honey, where are you?

Other words which can replace 당신 in this usage are 여보 (most common) and 자기 (more common among young couples).

Usage 5

This is becoming more and more rare. Often at times, people drop the word 당신 simply out of fear of being misunderstood.

Then, how do you say "you" in Korean?

Track 09

When speaking in 반말, you can say 너.

너 + 는 [topic marker] = 너는
너 + 가 [subject marker] = 네가 (written) or 니가 (spoken)

If speaking in 존댓말, simply say the name of the other person and add dependent nouns such as 씨, 님, or a word which describes his or her position or job title.

Ex)
현우 씨 지금 시간 있어요?

= (Talking to 현우) Do you have time now?

최경은 선생님, 어디예요?

= (Talking to teacher 최경은) Where are you?

Learn to Compare, Contrast, Modify,

If speaking in 존댓말, say the social status of the person.

Ex)

기사님, 여기에서 내려 주세요.

= (Talking to the taxi driver) Please drop me off here.

**Track
09**

Sample Dialogue

A: 당신 여권 가져왔어요?

B: 응, 가져왔지. 당신은?

A: 네, 저도 챙겼어요.

A: *Have you brought your passport, honey?*

B: *Yes, of course I have. How about you?*

A: *Yes, I have it with me as well.*

Learn to Compare, Contrast, Modify,

✏ Exercises for Lesson 5

Decide whether the statement is true or false, then circle or underline the appropriate answer.

1. You can use the word 당신 when happy with someone and you do not want to fight with that person.

   a. True   b. False

2. You can use the word 당신 when translating from a foreign language and a word for "you" is absolutely needed.

   a. True   b. False

3. You can use the word 당신 when writing or singing a song.

   a. True   b. False

Check the answers on **p.188**

4. You can use the word 당신 when addressing your parents.

   a. True   b. False

5. You can use the word 당신 when talking about someone (who is not present) in an honorific way, and you want to say "he" or "she".

   a. True   b. False

LESSON **6**

Word Builder 3

동(動)

Track 11

This lesson offers you a break from Korean grammar and allows you to focus more on vocabulary. With these Word Builder lessons, many (not all) of the words, or word elements, are based on Chinese characters (한자) but the meanings can differ from modern-day Chinese. You do not have to memorize all the vocabulary in this lesson, as it simply serves to help you understand how the key word element helps gives words their meaning.

The key word element of this lesson is 동.

The Chinese character for this word is 動.

The word element 동 is related to "movement", "move", and "to move".

Sample Expressions

운 (to transport) + 동 (to move) = 운동 運動 = exercise; workout

38

Ex)

요즘에 운동 열심히 하고 있어요.

= I have been diligently exercising lately.

동 (to move) + 작 (to make) = 동작 動作 = movement; move

Ex)

이 동작을 따라 하세요.

= Follow me and do this move.

작 (to make) + 동 (to move) = 작동 作動 = operation (of a device)

Ex)

작동이 안 돼요.

= It does not work.

Track 11

활 (to flow, to be alive) + 동 (to move) = 활동 活動 = activity

Ex)

온라인 활동

= online activities

음악 활동

= music/musical activities

TV 활동

= TV activities/appearances

동 (to move) + 사 (language) = [grammar term] 동사 動詞 = verb

39

Ex)

이 단어는 동사예요.

= This word is a verb.

동 (to move) + 물 (object, material) = 동물 動物 = animal

Ex)

동물 좋아해요?

= Do you like animals?

연 (to connect) + 동 (to move) = [internet term] 연동 聯動 = linkage; interlocking

Track 11

Ex)

페이스북 연동

= connecting to Facebook through another site

연동 되어 있어요.

= (Two web services) are linked/connected together.

행 (to do, to go) + 동 (to move) = 행동 行動 = behavior

Ex)

행동 똑바로 하세요!

= Behave yourself!

동 (to move) + 영 (to project) + 상 (image) = 동영상 動映像 = video

Ex)

동영상 응답

= video response

40

Sample Dialogue

Track 12

A: 주연 씨가 좋아하는 가수는 왜 요즘 활동을 안 해요?

B: 그래도 콘서트는 계속 하고 있어요.

A: 아, 그래요? 몰랐어요.

A: *Why hasn't the singer you like been doing anything these days, Jooyeon?*

B: *He has been holding concerts, though.*

A: *Oh, has he? I didn't know.*

41

✎ Exercises for Lesson 6

Fill in the blanks with the appropriate Sino-Korean word:

1. The word element (   ) is related to "movement", "move", and "to move".

2. exercise; workout

(   )

3. operation (of a device)

(   )

4. animal

(   )

5. video

(   )

Check the answers on **p.188**

42

LESSON 7

It is okay. / I am okay.

괜찮아요.

The expression **괜찮아요** is used in everyday Korean conversations and is most commonly translated to English as "It is okay" or "I am okay". Depending on the context of the sentence, 괜찮아요 can have various meanings beyond just "okay".

Track 13

괜찮아요 actually comes from a much longer sentence that does not quite make sense in its entirety.

Take a look at the phrase broken down below:

괜하다

= to be pointless; to be meaningless. (This word is almost never used by itself like this.)

괜하 + -지 않다* → 괜하지 않다 → 괜치 않다 → 괜찮다 = It is okay.

* Look back at Level 1, Lesson 21 if you have forgotten what this means!

Present tense ＝ 괜찮아요.

Past tense ＝ 괜찮았어요.

Future tense ＝ 괜찮을 거예요.

Now that you know a little more about 괜찮아요, complete this lesson by taking a look at some examples of how it can be used.

Usages of 괜찮아요

I.

I am okay.

I am alright.

Everything is fine.

Ex)

(You slip and fall on the ground, and someone asks you if you are alright.)

괜찮아요. ＝ I am okay.

2.

Do not worry.

No worries.

Ex)

(Your friend is worrying about something, and you want to tell her not to worry.)

괜찮아요. ＝ Do not worry.

3.

It is good.

> **Ex)**
>
> (You refer to something as "cool", "good", or "recommendable".)
>
> 이 영화 진짜 괜찮아요. = This movie is really good.

4.

I am cool.

I am good.

No, thanks.

> **Ex)**
>
> (Your friend offers you a drink, and you want to politely refuse it.)
>
> 괜찮아요. = No, thanks. I am good.

and Describe More Fluently in Korean!

Sample Dialogue

A: 석진 씨, 기침이 심한 것 같은데, 괜찮아요?

B: 괜찮아요. 목에 뭐가 걸려서 그래요.

A: 물을 좀 마실래요?

A: *Seokjin, it seems that you cough too much. Are you alright?*

B: *I'm fine. It's because there is something in my throat.*

A: *Do you want to drink some water?*

Learn to Compare, Contrast, Modify,

✏ Exercises for Lesson 7

Fill in the blanks by conjugating the word **괜찮다** *into its appropriate form.*

1. Heecheol, do you feel alright?

= 희철 씨, 몸은 좀 ( )?

2. Do not worry. It will be okay.

= 걱정하지 마세요. ( ).

3. This movie was really good.

= 이 영화 진짜 ( ).

4. (When someone offers you something) No, thanks.

= ( ).

Check the answers on **p.188**

47

LESSON 8

It is okay to..., You do not have to...

-아/어/여도 돼요, 안 -아/어/여도 돼요

Track 15

To say something such as "it is okay to..." or "you do not have to/need to..." in Korean, you will need to learn and use the following verb ending: **-아/어/여도 되다**

How it works:

되다 means "to function", "to be possible", or "can do".

> **Ex)**
> 지금 인터넷 돼요?
> = Does the Internet work now?
> 지금 배달 돼요?
> = Can you deliver the food now? / Is food delivery available now?
> 배달 돼요?
> = Do you deliver food as well? / Can food delivery be done?

Learn to Compare, Contrast, Modify,

도 means "also" or "too" (when used with nouns).

Ex)

저도 갈 거예요.

= I am going to go, too.

저도요.

= Me, too.

이것도 주세요.

= Give me this one, too.

-아/어/여 + -도 means "even if" or "even when" (when used with verb stems).

Ex)

먹어도 = even if you eat

몰라도 = even when you do not know

가도 = even if you go

해도 = even if you do

자도 = even if you sleep

일어나도 = even when you wake up

Track
15

When combined,
-아/어/여 + -도 + 되다 = -아/어/여도 되다 means "it is okay to..." or "it is okay even if you...".

Examples

(1)
켜다 = to turn on; to switch on

49

켜도 되다 = it is okay to turn... on; it is okay even if you switch... on

켜도 돼요. = It is okay. You can turn it on.

불 켜도 돼요. = You can turn the light on.

컴퓨터 켜도 돼요. = You can turn the computer on.

(2)

하다 = to do

해도 되다 = it is okay to do...; it is okay even if you do...

내일 해도 돼요. = It is okay if you do it tomorrow. / You can just do it tomorrow.

내일 해도 돼요? = Is it okay if I do it tomorrow?

(3)

시작하다 = to begin; to start

시작해도 되다 = it is okay to start

시작해도 돼요. = You can start.

시작해도 돼요? = Can I start? / Can we start?

Track 15

Sample Sentences

이거 나중에 해도 돼요.

= You can do this later.

(Question form: 이거 나중에 해도 돼요? = Can I do this later?)

컴퓨터 써도 돼요?

= May I use the computer?

오늘 쉬어도 돼요.

= You can take a day off today.

50

How to say "do not have to..."

By using the same structure (-아/어/여 + -도 + 되다) and adding 안 in front of it, you can say "do not have to..." or "it is not necessary to...".

Ex)

(1) 해도 돼요.

   = You can do it. / It is okay if you do it.

   안 해도 돼요.

   = You do not have to do it. / It is okay if you do not do it.

   청소 안 해도 돼요.

   = You do not have to clean up. / It is okay if you do not clean up.

   오늘 일 안 해도 돼요.

   = You do not have to work today. / It is okay if you do not work today.

Track 15

(2) 먹어도 돼요.

   = You can eat it. / It is okay if you eat it.

   안 먹어도 돼요.

   = You do not have to eat it. / It is okay if you do not eat it.

   안 마셔도 돼요.

   = You do not have to drink. / It is okay if you do not drink.

안 + -아/어/여 + -도 + 되다 does NOT translate to "you should not..." in English. However, the next lesson (Level 4, Lesson 9) will cover how to say "you should not" in Korean.

Sample Dialogue

A: 이거 차 트렁크에 넣어도 돼요?

B: 네.

A: 안 깨질까요?

B: 괜찮을 거예요.

A: Can I put this in the back of the car?

B: Yes.

A: You don't think it will get broken?

B: It will be fine.

Learn to Compare, Contrast, Modify,

🖉 Exercises for Lesson *8*

Translate the following sentences to Korean:

1. "You can turn the computer on."

( )

2. "Is it okay if I do it tomorrow?"

( )

3. "You can do this later."

( )

4. "You do not have to eat it."

( )

5. "You do not have to cut it."

( )

Check the answers on **p.189**

and Describe More Fluently in Korean!

LESSON 9

You should not…, You are not supposed to…

-(으)면 안 돼요

Track 17

In the previous lesson, you looked at how to use the -아/어/여도 되다 ending to tell someone that it is okay to do something or that he/she does not need/have to do something. In this lesson, you will learn the opposite: how to say "you should not…" or "you are not supposed to…" in Korean.

Conjugation

Verb stem + -(으)면 안 되다

-(으)면 안 되다 can be broken into two parts: -(으)면 and 안 되다. -(으) 면 means "if" (go to Level 2, Lesson 23 to review this), and 되다 means "to work", "to function", "to be possible", or "can do". Therefore, 안 되다 means "it cannot be done", "it is not possible", or "it is not okay".

-(으)면 안 되다 literally means "it is not okay if…" or "it is not acceptable if…", and it can be more naturally translated to "you should not…" or "you are not supposed to…" in English.

54

Examples

1. 열다 = to open

열면 안 돼요.

= You should not open it. / You are not supposed to open it.

열면 안 돼요?

= Should I not open it? / Am I not supposed to open it?

열면 안 돼.

= [to a child] You should not open it.

열어도 돼요.

= It is okay to open it. / You can go ahead and open it.

열어도 돼요?

= Can I open it?

Track 17

2. 만지다 = to touch

만지면 안 돼요.

= You should not touch it. / You cannot touch it.

만지면 안 돼요?

= [asking for permission] Am I not supposed to touch it?

만지면 안 돼.

= [to a child] You should not touch it.

만져도 돼요.

= It is okay to touch it. / You can go ahead and touch it.

만져도 돼요?

= Can I touch it?

55

More Verb Conjugation: Practice

I. 던지다 = to throw

던지면 안 돼요.

= You should not throw it.

던져도 돼요.

= It is okay to throw it.

2. 팔다 = to sell

팔면 안 돼요.

= You should not sell it.

팔아도 돼요.

= It is okay to sell it.

Track
17

3. 말하다 = to tell; to talk

말하면 안 돼요.

= You should not tell/talk.

말해도 돼요.

= It is okay to tell/talk.

Sample Sentences

지금 말하면 안 돼요?

= Shouldn't I tell/talk now? / Am I not supposed to tell/talk now?

여기서 팔면 안 돼요?

= Shouldn't I sell it here? / Am I not supposed to sell it here?

그거 던지면 안 돼요. 유리예요.

= You should not throw it. It is (made of) glass.

Track 17

and Describe More Fluently in Korean!

A: 불 켜면 안 돼요. 아기가 자고 있어요.

B: 아, 그럼 텔레비전 봐도 돼요?

A: 텔레비전도 보면 안 돼요.

A: *You shouldn't turn the light on. The baby is sleeping.*

B: *Oh, then is it okay to watch TV?*

A: *You shouldn't watch TV either.*

Learn to Compare, Contrast, Modify,

✏ Exercises for Lesson 9

Write the following sentences in Korean:

1. "You are not supposed to open it."

( )

2. "Am I not supposed to touch it?"

( )

3. "You cannot go in there."

( )

Check the answers on **p.189**

4. "Am I not supposed to tell/talk now?"

( )

5. "You should not throw it."

( )

LESSON **10**

Among, Between

중에서, 사이에서, 사이에

Track 19

To say things such as "I cannot choose between this one and that one" or "she is popular among our friends" in Korean, you need to learn to use **중에서**, **사이에서**, or **사이에**.

Start this lesson with learning about 중에서!

The Chinese character is 中, which means "center" or "middle". -에서 is a way to mark a location; therefore, when 중 and -에서 are together, it literally means "in the middle".

Other words which contain 중 (中) are:

중학교 = 중 (middle) + 학교 (school) = middle school
중식 = 중 (middle) + 식 (eat) = formal name for "lunch"
회의 중 = 회의 (meeting, conference) + 중 (middle) = meeting in progress
공사 중 = 공사 (construction) + 중 (middle) = under construction

Learn to Compare, Contrast, Modify,

중에서 means "among" or "between", but it can only be used when listing a few options to choose from. You CANNOT use 중에서 to describe a location and say something such as "the house is located between the bank and the park". In that case, a different expression, 사이에, is needed (and is explained later in this lesson).

Expression (1) - 중에서

* To make 중에서 shorter, you can drop 서.

When choosing from a few options, put 중에서 at the end of "A and B".

Track 19

Ex)

Between A and B
= A하고 B 중에서

Between this book and that book
= 이 책하고 저 책 중에서

Among these three things
= 이 세 개 중에서

Among ten people
= 열 명 중에서

Sample Sentences

Please choose among these.
= 이 중에서 고르세요.

61

Please take one of these three.

= 이 세 개 중에서 하나 가져가세요.

Expression (2) – 사이에서

When saying "among", such as in "popular among friends" or "famous among teenagers", use the expression 사이에서. 사이 can refer to a relationship or the theoretical space between certain objects or people.

Track 19

Ex)
Among friends

= 친구들 사이에서

Among his/her family members

= 가족들 사이에서

Sample Sentences

He is popular among friends.

= 친구들 사이에서 인기가 많아요.

This singer is popular among Koreans.

= 이 가수는 한국인들 사이에서 인기가 많아요.

Seokjin is popular among our listeners.

= 석진 씨는 청취자들 사이에서 인기가 많아요.

62

Expression (3) – 사이에

사이에 is used to refer to the physical space between two objects or people.

Sample Sentences

I am between the bank and the park.

= 은행하고 공원 사이에 있어요.

The pharmacy is between the school and the police station.

= 약국은 학교하고 경찰서 사이에 있어요.

Q : What is the difference between -에 and -에서?

A : -에 is used to mark status or location, and -에서 is used for an action.

Track 19

Sample Dialogue

A: 현정 씨, 재미있는 책 좀 추천해
주세요.

B: 저는 소설책만 읽어서 소설책밖에
몰라요.

A: 괜찮아요. 소설책 중에서 재미있는
거 알려 주세요.

A: *Hyeonjeong, please recommend some
interesting books.*

B: *I only read novels, so I only know
about novels.*

A: *That's okay. Among novels, please let
me know about some interesting ones.*

Learn to Compare, Contrast, Modify,

✏️ Exercises for Lesson *10*

Complete each sentence by filling in the blank with **중에서**, **사이에서**, *or* **사이에**.

1. 은행하고 공원 (　　　　　) 있어요. = I am between the bank and the park.

2. 꼭 이 (　　　　　) 골라야 돼요? = Do I have to choose among these?

3. 이 가수는 한국인들 (　　　　　) 인기가 많아요. = This singer is popular among Koreans.

4. 이 (　　　　　) 뭐가 끼였어요. = Something is stuck between my teeth.

5. 페이스북이 대학생들 (　　　　　) 유행이에요. = Facebook is all the rage among college students.

Check the answers on **p.189**

BLOG

Imjingak - Pyeonghwanuri Park
(임진각 평화누리 공원)

Believe it or not, there is more to Korea than just Seoul. Although Seoul seems to be where most of the "action" is happening, there are great things in other parts of Korea that few people experience because they are unaware of their existence. For example, near the DMZ and just 100 meters from 임진강역 (Imjingang Station) in Gyeonggi-do, there is a beautiful park called 평화누리 공원.

임진강역 and 평화누리 공원 are near the town of 임진각, which is on the outskirts of the DMZ. Actually, it is only 7 kilometers (a little over 4 miles) away from the DMZ, and it rests on the banks of the 임진강 (Imjin River) in 파주시 (Paju City). The town was built a couple of decades after the Korean War armistice and stands as a symbol of hope: that someday, reunification between the North and South will take place. Since the theme of reunification is so strong in this area, 평화누리 공원 was built in 2005 as part of a Global Peace Festival sponsored by Gyeonggi-do.

평화누리 공원 has a 바람의 언덕, which literally means a "hill for wind", and the 공원 is kind of famous for this particular spot due to the thousands of colorful 바람개비 (pinwheels). The 바람의 언덕 is an absolutely fantastic place to take photos, and if you are interested in capturing the movement of the 바람개비, make sure to use a slow shutter speed when snapping photos.

In Seoul, you cannot find such a space that is so wide and open like the one at 평화누리 공원. This 공원 is a super great place to go for the day to run around, walk, or to just simply hang out under the shade of a parasol with your family and friends enjoying the fresh air. You can also have a picnic-style gathering here, so make sure to load up with lots of 김밥 and 맥주!

There is actually a family of wild ducks that live near the outdoor stage which, amazingly, floats on water. On this outdoor stage, high-quality performances are held every Sunday and movies of various genres are shown on the screen daily. These cultural events (including the cute ducks and 바람개비) bring happiness to the eyes and ears of the onlookers, despite being so close to the spot where the pain and suffering of separated families still remains.

평화누리 공원 is about a 2 hour bus ride north of Seoul. No private cars or 택시 are allowed to access the park or the town of 임진각 because of its proximity to the DMZ, so it is best to catch a bus to get there.

We hope you are enjoying Level 4 so far!

Keep up the good work!

LESSON **11**

Any

아무 (Part 1)

To say "anyone", "anything", or "anywhere" in Korean, the word that you need to remember is 아무.

아무 basically means "any" in a positive context, and it HAS TO be used along with other nouns - no exceptions! When it is used in a negative context, it means "no" + noun.

Sample Expressions (positive sentences)

For positive sentences, add -나 at the end of the word.

1. **아무나** = anybody; does not matter who; anyone

 Ex)
 아무나 올 수 있어요. = Anyone can come.

70

2. **아무거나** = anything; does not matter what

> **Ex)**
> 아무거나 주세요. = Just give me anything.
> (아무거나 comes from 아무 + 것이나. 것 means "thing".)

3. **아무 데나** = anywhere; any place

> **Ex)**
> 아무 데나 좋아요. = Any place is good.
> (In the dictionary, 데 means "place" or "spot".)

Sample Expressions (negative sentences)

Track
21

For negative sentences, add -도 at the end of the word.

1. **아무도** = nobody; not anybody

> **Ex)**
> 아무도 없어요? = Nobody is here?

2. **아무것도** = nothing; not anything

> **Ex)**
> 아무것도 만지지 마세요. = Do not touch anything.
> 아무것도 몰라요. = I do not know anything.

3. **아무 데도** = nowhere; not any place

Ex)

아무 데도 안 갈 거예요. = I am not going anywhere.

How to say "not just anything/anyone/anywhere"

If you want someone to be careful making a choice when saying something such as "Do not hang out with just anyone", "Do not buy just anything", or "Do not eat just anywhere", use the expression 아무나 (anyone), 아무거나 (anything), or 아무 데나 (anywhere).

Track 21

Ex)

(1) 아무나 올 수 없어요.

= Not everyone can come.

아무도 올 수 없어요.

= Nobody can come.

(2) 아무거나 먹으면 안 돼요.

= You should not eat just anything.

아무것도 먹으면 안 돼요.

= You should not eat anything at all.

(3) 아무 데나 가고 싶지 않아요.

= I do not want to go just anywhere.

아무 데도 가고 싶지 않아요.

= I do not want to go anywhere.

72

There are more types of expressions using 아무, such as 아무때나 for "anytime" and 아무한테나 for "to anyone", but those will be covered in a future lesson.

Sample Dialogue

A: 왜 벌써 왔어요?

B: 가게에 아무도 없어서 머리를 못 잘랐어요.

A: 다른 데 아무 데나 가면 안 돼요?

B: 안 돼요. 거기서 잘라야 돼요.

A: Why are you back already?

B: There was nobody at the shop, so I couldn't get my hair cut.

A: Can't you just go to any other shop?

B: No, it's not possible. I have to get my hair done there.

Learn to Compare, Contrast, Modify,

✏ Exercises for Lesson 11

Choose one of the following which best completes each sentence: 아무나, 아무도, 아무거나, 아무것도, 아무 데나, *or* 아무 데도.

1. (   ) 가고 싶지 않아요. = I do not want to go anywhere.

2. (   ) 올 수 있어요. = Anybody can come.

3. (   ) 만지지 마세요. = Do not touch anything.

4. (   ) 몰라요. = Nobody knows.

5. (   ) 주세요. = Give me just anything.

Check the answers on **p.189**

and Describe More Fluently in Korean!

LESSON **12**

To try doing something

-아/어/여 보다

Track 23

This particular sentence structure "verb stem + **-아/어/여 보다**" is used to:

1. tell someone to try or attempt something;

2. ask if someone has ever done or tried something;

3. make a command sound less demanding.

The structure -아/어/여 보다 is composed of two parts: -아/어/여 and 보다. -아/어/여 is the basic suffix used after verb stems, and 보다 means "to see". The literal translation of -아/어/여 보다 is "to do something and see (what happens)".

Nevertheless, this structure really does not have a specific meaning and is used simply to make sentences more natural. However, the most common translation of -아/어/여 보다 is "to try doing something".

Conjugation

Verb stem + -아/어/여 보다

Examples

(1) 쓰다 = to use

  → 쓰 + -어 보다 = 써 보다 = to try using (something)

이거 써 봤어요?

= Have you tried using this? / Have you used this before?

(2) 들어가다 = to enter, to go in

  → 들어가 + -아 보다 = 들어가 보다 = to try going in

들어가 볼까요?

= Shall we try going in (and see what it is like)? / Shall we attempt to go in?

Track
23

(3) 하다 = to do

  → 하 + -여 보다 = 해 보다 = to try doing (something)

이거 해 보고 싶어요.

= I want to try doing this. / I want to give it a try.

Fixed expressions and verbs containing -아/어/여 보다

Since -아/어/여 보다 is a frequently used structure, some verbs are more common in the
-아/어/여 보다 structure than others, and other verbs are actually already in the form of
-아/어/여 보다. For some structures, -아/어/여 보다 is already a part of some verbs, so the
space between -아/어/여 and 보다 is not necessary.

77

1. 물어보다 vs 물어 보다

- 물어보다 = to ask; to try asking

- 물어 보다 (x)

2. 알아보다 vs 알아 보다

- 알아보다 = to look into something; to recognize

- 알아 보다 (x)

3. 지켜보다 vs 지켜 보다

- 지켜보다 = to keep a watchful eye on someone/something

- 지켜 보다 (x)

Track 23

Sample Sentences

이거 먹어 봐요.

= Try eating this. / Try some of this.

저도 거기 안 가 봤어요.

= I have not been there yet, either. / I have not tried going there, either.

제가 먼저 해 볼게요.

= I will try doing it first. / I will give it a try first.

누구한테 물어볼까요?

= Whom shall I ask?

제가 알아볼게요.

= I will look into it.

Learn to Compare, Contrast, Modify,

Sample Dialogue

Track
24

A: 핸드폰을 잃어버렸어요.

B: 언제요?

A: 모르겠어요.

B: 전화를 한번 걸어 보세요.

A: *I've lost my phone.*

B: *When?*

A: *I don't know.*

B: *Please try making a phone call.*

and Describe More Fluently in Korean!

✏ Exercises for Lesson 12

Translate each phrase to Korean and write it on the lines provided below:

1. Have you tried using this?

....

2. Shall we try going in (to see what it is like)?

....

3. Whom shall I ask?

....

4. I will look into it.

....

5. I want to try doing this.

....

Check the answers on **p.189**

Learn to Compare, Contrast, Modify,

LESSON **13**

Word Builder 4

불(不)

부/불, which is written as 不 in Hanja, is the foundation for many useful words which are used every single day in Korean conversations.

Track 25

부/불 (不) means "not" in English.

Sample Expressions

불 (not) + 안 (comfortable; relaxed) = 불안 不安 = anxiety; anxious

    Ex)
    불안해하지 마세요. = Do not be anxious.

불 (not) + 편 (comfortable; convenient) = 불편 不便 = inconvenient; uncomfortable

    Ex)
    불편해요. = It is inconvenient. / It is uncomfortable.

81

불 (not) + 완전 (complete) = 불완전 不完全 = incomplete

Ex)
불완전한 정보 = incomplete information

불 (not) + 균형 (balance) = 불균형 不均衡 = imbalance

Ex)
성비 불균형 = gender ratio imbalance

불 (not) + 만 (full) = 불만 不滿 = complaint

Track 25

Ex)
저한테 불만 있어요? = Do you have any complaints against me?

不 (불) is pronounced and written as 부 when the consonant that follows is either ㄷ or ㅈ.

Sample Expressions

부 (not) + 정확 (correct) = 부정확 不正確 = incorrect; inaccurate

Ex)
부정확한 발음
= inaccurate pronunciation

부 (not) + 주의 (attention) = 부주의 不注意 = carelessness

82

Ex)

제 부주의로 사고가 났어요.

= I was careless, so it caused an accident. / My carelessness caused an accident.

부 (not) + 당 (correct, right) = 부당 不當 = wrong; unfair; unjust

Ex)

부당한 일을 당했어요. = Someone did something unfair to me.

부 (not) + 적절 (proper) = 부적절 不適切 = inappropriate

Ex)

부적절한 예문 = inappropriate example sentence

Track 25

* Note

When 부 is understood as 副, it means "assistant", "deputy", or "vice" as in "vice president".

Sample Dialogue

Track 26

A: 그 포스터 어떻게 붙였어요?

B: 테이프로 붙였어요.

A: 떨어지지 않을까요? 불안해요.

A: How did you stick the poster up?

B: I stuck it up with tape.

A: Don't you think it will fall off? It doesn't look stable.

✎ *Exercises for Lesson* **13**

1. The word element (   ) means "not" in English.

Write the following words in Korean. All given words are Sino-Korean.

2. Complaint

(   )

3. Incorrect; inaccurate

(   )

4. Inappropriate

(   )

5. Inconvenient; uncomfortable

(   )

Check the answers on **p.189**

LESSON 14

Sometimes, Often, Always, Seldom, Never

가끔, 자주, 항상, 별로, 전혀

Track 27

To form a sentence which uses adverbs of frequency (빈도 부사) in Korean - such as "seldom", "almost", or "always" - it is important to not only memorize the words, but to also actually practice using them along with the verbs used in conjunction with 빈도 부사.

Take a look at some 빈도 부사 in Korean:

- **가끔** = sometimes
- **자주** = often

- **항상** = always [more common in written language]
- **맨날** = (lit. every day), always; all the time [more common in spoken language]

- **별로** = seldom; rarely
- **전혀** = not at all
- **거의** = almost (but) not at all

86

Where do 빈도 부사 fit in a sentence?

These 빈도 부사 usually go right before the verb of a sentence, but unlike in English, their position is very flexible. As long as the meaning of your sentence is clear, it does not matter where they are placed. You can, however, emphasize a certain part of a sentence by changing the word order and intonation.

Sample Sentences

가끔 서점에 가요.

= I sometimes go to the bookstore.

= 서점에 가끔 가요. (The speaker might be emphasizing 가끔 here.)

Track 27

자주 한국 영화 봐요.

= I often watch Korean movies.

= 한국 영화 자주 봐요. (The speaker might be emphasizing 자주 here.)

그런 말 정말 자주 들어요.

= I hear that really often.

= I get that really often.

항상 물어보고 싶었어요.

= I have always wanted to ask you (that).

중국어를 맨날 공부하는데, 아직 어려워요.

= I study Chinese all the time, but it is still difficult.

요즘에는 운동을 별로 안 해요.

= I rarely work out these days.

= These days, I seldom work out.

= These days, I do not work out that often.

화장을 전혀 안 해요.

= I do not put on makeup at all.

= I never put on makeup.

= I do not put on any makeup at all.

시간이 없어서, 친구들을 거의 못 만나요.

= I do not have time, so I can hardly meet my friends.

Track 27

라디오를 거의 맨날 들어요.

= I listen to the radio almost every day.

Learn to Compare, Contrast, Modify,

Sample Dialogue

Track 28

A: 경은 씨는 이상형이 있어요?

B: 저는 자주 바뀌어요. 주연 씨는요?

A: 저는 항상 똑같아요. 잘 웃는 사람이요.

A: *Do you have any ideal type, Kyeong-eun?*

B: *My type often changes. How about you, Jooyeon?*

A: *My ideal type has always been the same. Someone who smiles a lot.*

and Describe More Fluently in Korean!

🖉 Exercises for Lesson 14

Match each Korean word with its English translation.

1. 별로   a. often

2. 거의   b. always [more common in written language]

3. 항상   c. (lit. every day), always [more common in spoken language]

4. 가끔   d. almost not at all

5. 맨날   e. not at all

6. 전혀   f. sometimes

7. 자주   g. seldom, rarely

Check the answers on **p.189**

Learn to Compare, Contrast, Modify,

LESSON 15

Any

아무 (Part 2)

Track
29

In Lesson 11 of this level, you were already introduced to some expressions relating to 아무, which included: 아무나 (anybody), 아무거나 (anything), 아무 데나 (anywhere), 아무도 (nobody), 아무것도 (nothing), and 아무 데도 (nowhere). Building upon that knowledge, you will now learn a few more expressions which are related to 아무 in this lesson.

1. 아무 때나

= just anytime; anytime

= 아무 (any) + 때 (moment, time) + -나

> **Ex)**
> 아무 때나 한국어 공부할 수 있어요. = You can study Korean anytime.

2. 아무 말도 / 아무 이야기도

= no word; no mention

= 아무 (any) + 말/이야기 (language/word) + -도 (even/also)

91

Ex)

아무 말도 하지 마세요. = Please do not say a word.

3. 아무렇지도 않다

= to be alright; to be okay; to be unaffected by

= 아무 (any) + 그렇다 (to be so) + -지 않다 (to be not)

* This expression only works in a negative format.

Ex)

저는 아무렇지도 않아요. = I am okay.

4. 아무한테도

= to nobody

Track 29

= 아무 (anybody) + -한테 (to) + -도 (even/also)

Ex)

아무한테도 주지 말고 혼자 먹어요. = Do not share this with anyone, and (only) eat it alone.

5. 아무렇게나

= just in any way; however you like it

* Here, 아무렇게 is like an adverb, but it does not work independently. It ONLY works in this format.

Ex)

아무렇게나 하지 마세요. = Please do not just do it any way you want.

6. 아무(런) + noun + -도 + (없어요)

= there is no + noun (of any kind)

Learn to Compare, Contrast, Modify,

Ex)

아무(런) 소식도 없어요. = There is no news (from them).

* If you are talking about news that you see on TV or in newspapers, it is 뉴스 in Korean.

The news that you hear from your friends or family is 소식.

* Fixed expression

아무것도 아니에요. = It is nothing.

**Track
29**

93

Sample Dialogue

Track 30

A: 요즘 잠을 잘 못 자요. 밤에 침대에 누워도 잠이 안 와요.

B: 진짜요? 저는 아무 때나 잘 수 있는데.

A: 아무 때나요?

B: 네. 저는 낮에도 침대에 누우면 바로 잠들어요.

A: I don't sleep well these days. Even when I lie in bed, I can't sleep.

B: Really? In my case, I can sleep anytime.

A: Anytime?

B: Yes. Even during the day, if I lie in bed, I go to sleep right away.

Learn to Compare, Contrast, Modify,

🖊 Exercises for Lesson 15

Fill in the blanks with an appropriate conjugation of 아무.

1. Please do not just do it whatever way you want. = (   ) 하지 마세요.

2. It is nothing. = (   ) 아니에요.

3. It is tasteless. = (   ) 없어요. *taste = 맛

4. Do not give it to anybody. = (   ) 주지 마세요.

5. Please do not say any word. = (   ) 하지 마세요. *word = 말

Check the answers on **p.190**

LESSON **16**

Spacing in Korean

띄어쓰기 (Part I)

When writing in Korean, in order to avoid unclear and confusing sentences, it is important to understand the use of spacing.

Spacing rules in Korean

Spacing (띄어쓰기) in Korean is similar to, but still very different from, English. In terms of words, independent words can be written separately (with a space between two words), but there are some cases in which you should NOT have a space between two words.

There should be a space between:

1. an adjective and a noun

> **Ex)**
> 예쁜 강아지 = a pretty puppy

Learn to Compare, Contrast, Modify,

부지런한 사람 = a hardworking person

2. an adverb and a verb

Ex)

조용히 걷다 = to walk quietly

빨리 말하다 = to speak fast

3. a noun (+ marker) and a verb

Ex)

이거(를) 샀어요. = I bought this.

그것(을) 만들었어요. = I made it.

Track
31

4. a noun and another noun

Ex)

한국 여행 = trip to Korea

지갑 가격 = the cost of a wallet

There is no space between:

1. a noun/pronoun and a marker

Ex)

저 + 는 = 저는 = I + subject marker

저 + 를 = 저를 = I + object marker

2. nouns in a proper name (if it has been decided that the name is to be in that format)

Ex)

한국관광공사 = Korea Tourism Organization

서울도시철도공사 = Seoul Metropolitan Rapid Transit

Exceptions

1. Words which form fixed expressions can be written together without space.

Ex)

이 + 것 = 이 것 → 이것

가족 + 사진 = 가족 사진 → 가족사진

* These two words are put together because they are commonly used together.

** This lack of spacing is commonly found in Sino-Korean words.

2. Noun + 하다

- 공부(를) 하다 = 공부 하다 → 공부하다

- 운동(을) 하다 = 운동 하다 → 운동하다

- 청소(를) 하다 = 청소 하다 → 청소하다

Sample Dialogue

A: 예쁜 꽃이 정말 많네요.

B: 다 사고 싶어요.

A: 어떤 꽃을 살까요?

B: 음... 이거요!

A: *There are so many pretty flowers!*

B: *I would like to buy them all.*

A: *Which flower shall we buy?*

B: *Hmm... this one!*

and Describe More Fluently in Korean!

🖉 Exercises for Lesson 16

Correct the spacing of each phrase. If it is correct, leave it as it is and write it again on the spaces provided.

1. 부지런한사람 (= a hardworking person) → ....

2. 이거샀어요. (= I bought this.) → ....

3. 한국여행 (= trip to Korea) → ....

4. 한국관광공사 (= Korea Tourism Organization) → ....

5. 빨리말해요. (= Speak fast.) → ....

Check the answers on **p.190**

Learn to Compare, Contrast, Modify,

LESSON **17**

Word Contractions - Topic/Subject marker

축약형 (Part I) - 주격 조사

In the previous lesson, you just barely scratched the surface of spacing rules in Korean. By digging a bit deeper, you can learn about some more common word contractions.

Track 33

Topic marker contractions

When topic markers are used after nouns and pronouns, sometimes they are shortened so people can speak faster.

1. 저는 → 전 [polite]

> **Ex)**
> 저는 괜찮아요. = I am alright. → 전 괜찮아요.

2. 나는 → 난 [casual]

> **Ex)**
> 나는 여기 있을게. = I will stay here. → 난 여기 있을게.

101

3. 이것은 [very formal] → 이거는 [casual] → 이건 [casual]

Ex)

이것은 뭐예요? = What is this? → 이건 뭐예요?

4. 서울에는 → 서울엔

Ex)

서울에는 왜 왔어요? = What brings you to Seoul? → 서울엔 왜 왔어요?

5. 어제는 → 어젠

Ex)

어제는 왜 안 왔어요? = Why didn't you come yesterday? → 어젠 왜 안 왔어요?

Track
33

Subject marker contractions

When the subject marker -이 is used after 것, it is contracted to 게.

1. 이것이 [formal] → 이게 [casual]

Ex)

이것이 좋아요. = This one is good. → 이게 좋아요.

2. 저것이 [formal] → 저게 [casual]

Ex)

저것이 더 예뻐요. = That (over there) is prettier. → 저게 더 예뻐요.

3. 그것이 [formal] → 그게 [casual]

Ex)

그것이 어디 있어요? = Where is it? → 그게 어디 있어요?

* *You can use these shortened forms anytime except in extremely formal situations.*

Sample Sentences

전 학생이에요.

= I am a student.

이건 제 거예요.

= This is mine.

Track 33

서울엔 눈이 오고 있어요.

= (Well, in other areas I do not know, but) As far as Seoul is concerned, it is snowing.

어젠 뭐 했어요?

= What did you do yesterday?

저게 편해요.

= That is convenient. / There are no other things as convenient as that one.

저는 그게 없어요.

= I do not have it.

103

Sample Dialogue

A: 어젠 왜 울었어요?

B: 아무것도 아니에요.

A: 무슨 일인데요? 말해 보세요.

B: 다음에 얘기해 줄게요.

A: Why did you cry yesterday?

B: It's nothing.

A: What happened? Tell me.

B: I will tell you next time.

✏ Exercises for Lesson 17

Turn each of the following Korean words into contractions:

I. 이것은 →

2. 너는 →

3. 어제는 →

4. 여기는 →

5. 그것이 →

Check the answers on **p.190**

and Describe More Fluently in Korean!

LESSON **18**

The most

제일, 가장

Track 35

Most (+ adjective/adverb) = **제일/가장**

In English, the words "most" and "best" can be used as both adverbs and nouns. The usage you will look at in this lesson is its usage only as an adverb. (When "most" works as a noun, other Korean words are used, and they will be introduced in a future lesson.)

제일 and 가장 are almost the same thing and they can be used interchangeably. 제일 is a Sino-Korean word while 가장 is a native Korean word.

Examples

(1)
예쁘다 = to be pretty
제일 예뻐요. = (subject) is the prettiest/the most beautiful.
제일 예쁜 여자 = the prettiest girl/the most beautiful girl
제일 = 가장

Learn to Compare, Contrast, Modify,

제일 예뻐요 = 가장 예뻐요
제일 예쁜 여자 = 가장 예쁜 여자

* **제일** *is used more commonly in spoken Korean than* **가장**.

(2)
좋다 = to be good
제일 좋아요. = (subject) is the best (most + good).
제일 좋은 것 = the best (most + good) thing

Sample Sentences

이게 제일 좋아요.
= This is the best (one).

Track 35

제일 가까운 역이 어디예요?
= Where is the closest station?

어떤 색깔이 가장 좋아요?
= Which color is the best? / Which color is your favorite?

제일 먼저 온 사람이 누구예요?
= Who is the person that came here first?

요즘 가장 인기 있는 가수는 누구예요?
= These days, who is the most popular singer?

Sample Dialogue

Track 36

A: 신발이 너무 귀엽네요.

B: 저희 딸이 제일 좋아하는 신발이에요.

A: 아, 그래요?

B: 네. 핑크색을 제일 좋아해서 이것만 신어요.

A: Those shoes are so cute.

B: These are the shoes that my daughter likes the most.

A: Oh, are they?

B: Yes. Her favorite color is pink, so she only wears these.

Learn to Compare, Contrast, Modify,

✎ Exercises for Lesson 18

*1*a. What is the Korean word which means "the best" or "the most"? (Give two answers:)

(   )

*1*b. Which one is more colloquial?

(   )

Translate each phrase to Korean and write it on the lines provided below:

2. the prettiest girl

....

3. the best (most + good) thing

....

4. Where is the closest station?

....

Check the answers on **p.190**

LESSON 19

Less, Not completely

덜

Track 37

In previous Talk To Me In Korean lessons, you learned how to say "more" and "most". Do you remember? Yes? Great! This lesson will now teach you how to use "less" in Korean sentences to help you get your point across in a natural way.

$$덜 = less$$

While in English the word "less" can be used as a noun as well as an adverb or adjective, the Korean word 덜 can only be used as an adverb (modifying verbs only).

Ex)
덜 먹다 = to eat (something) less

In English, when saying "to eat less", it generally means that you are eating something, but you are eating less of that something. In Korean, however, the word 덜 is the object of the verb 먹다 which means that what you are actually doing is "less of the action" of 먹다. If

110

you translate 덜 먹다 into "to eat less" in English, the word "less" becomes a noun, which is not accurate. If you translate 덜 먹다 to "to eat (something) less", it becomes closer to the original meaning in Korean. If you are confused, do not worry! We will show you some examples.

Ex)
덜 쓰다 = to use (something) less
덜 춥다 = to be less cold
덜 비싸다 = to be less expensive

* Since verbs almost always come at the end of sentences in Korean, the word 덜 comes before verbs.

Track 37

Sample Sentences

어제보다 덜 추워요.

= It is less cold than yesterday.

덜 비싼 것 없어요?

= Don't you have a less expensive one?

물은 더 마시고, 밥은 덜 먹어야 돼요.

= (lit.) You should drink water more and eat less rice.

= You should drink more water and eat less.

덜 can also mean "not completely yet".

덜 basically means "less", but it can also mean "not fully" or "not completely yet". The opposite of this is 다, which means "all" or "completely".

111

Sample Conversations

A: 그 우유 다 마셨어요?

= Did you drink all of that milk?

B: 아니요. 다 안 마셨어요. 덜 마셨어요.

= No, I did not drink all of it. I have not finished it yet.

A: 다 왔어요?

= Are we there yet?

B: 덜 왔어요.

= We are not there yet.

Track 37

A: 제 책 돌려주세요.

= Give me my book back.

B: 아직 덜 봤어요.

= I have not finished it yet.

Learn to Compare, Contrast, Modify,

Sample Dialogue

A: 이 소설 무서워요?

B: 네. 그런데 낮에 읽으면 덜 무서워요.

A: 밤에 읽으면요?

B: 밤에 읽으면 진짜 무서워요.

A: Is this novel scary?

B: Yes, but if you read it during the day, it is less scary.

A: What if you read it at night?

B: If you read it at night, it is very scary.

113

✎ Exercises for Lesson 19

1. Which adverb means "less" in Korean?

( )

2. Translate "It is less cold than yesterday" to Korean.

( )

Use either 덜 *or* 다 *to fill in the blanks.*

Check the answers on **p.190**

3. A: 그 우유 .... 마셨어요? (= Did you drink all of that milk?)

B: 아니요. .... 안 마셨어요. .... 마셨어요. (= No, I did not drink all of it. I have not finished it yet.)

4. A: .... 왔어요? (= Are we there yet?)

B: .... 왔어요. (= We are not there yet.)

5. A: 제 책 돌려주세요. (= Give me my book back.)

B: 아직 .... 봤어요. (= I have not finished it yet.)

114

LESSON 20

Sentence Building Drill 1

Sentence Building Drill 1

Track 39

Hooray! You have made it to the first lesson of the "Sentence Building Drill" series! You have been introduced to many grammatical points thus far, so it is high time to put that knowledge to good use by training yourself to make Korean sentences more comfortably.

In these "Sentence Building Drill" lessons, you will be introduced to THREE key sentences, then you will practice changing different parts of the sentences so that you do not end up just memorizing the same three sentences. The goal is to be as comfortable and as flexible as possible when making Korean sentences.

Key sentence (1)

오늘부터 한국어를 더 열심히 공부할 거예요.

= Starting from today, I am going to study Korean harder.

Key sentence (2)

아마 내일부터 일요일까지 비가 내릴 거예요.

= It will probably rain from tomorrow until Sunday.

115

and Describe More Fluently in Korean!

Key sentence (3)

내일 시간이 있으면, 같이 커피 마실래요?

= If you have time tomorrow, will you drink coffee together (with me)?

Expansion & variation practice with key sentence (1)

Original sentence:

오늘부터 한국어를 더 열심히 공부할 거예요.

I.

오늘부터 = from today; starting from today

내일부터 = from tomorrow

지금부터 = from now on

언제부터? = since when?

2.

한국어를 공부할 거예요. = I am going to study Korean.

한국어를 연습할 거예요. = I am going to practice Korean.

한국어를 쓸 거예요. = I am going to use Korean.

한국어로* 말할 거예요. = I am going to talk in Korean.   * 한국어로 = in Korean

한국어를 배울 거예요. = I am going to learn Korean.

3.

열심히 공부할 거예요. = I am going to study hard.

열심히 일할 거예요. = I am going to work hard.

열심히 준비할 거예요. = I am going to prepare hard.

I am going to do my best with the preparation.

Learn to Compare, Contrast, Modify,

열심히 연습할 거예요 = I am going to practice hard

4.

열심히 공부하다 = to study hard

더 열심히 공부하다 = to study harder

덜 열심히 공부하다 = to study less hard

Expansion & variation practice with key sentence (2)

Original sentence:

아마 내일부터 일요일까지 비가 내릴 거예요.

1.

내일부터 일요일까지 = from tomorrow until Sunday

내일부터 모레까지 = from tomorrow until the day after tomorrow

어제부터 오늘까지 = from yesterday until today

지난주부터 다음 주까지 = from last week until next week

2.

비가 내릴 거예요. = It is going to rain.

비가 올 거예요. = It is going to rain.

눈이 내릴 거예요. = It is going to snow.

눈이 올 거예요. = It is going to snow.

비가 그칠* 거예요. = It is going to stop raining.   * 그치다 = to stop

눈이 그칠 거예요. = It is going to stop snowing.

비가 많이 내릴 거예요. = It is going to rain a lot.

눈이 많이 내릴 거예요. = It is going to snow a lot.

Track 39

117

3.

아마 비가 내릴 거예요. = It will probably rain.

분명히 비가 내릴 거예요. = It will certainly rain.

어쩌면 비가 내릴지도 몰라요. = Maybe it might rain.

어쩌면 비가 내릴 수도 있어요. = Maybe it could rain.

Expansion & variation practice with key sentence (3)

Original sentence:

내일 시간이 있으면, 같이 커피 마실래요?

Track
39

1.

시간이 있으면 = if you have time

시간이 없으면 = if you do not have time

시간이 *많이 있으면 = if you have a lot of time

* 많이 is an adverb which describes 있다.

시간이 *많으면 = if you have a lot of time

* 많다 here is used as a descriptive verb.

시간이 조금 밖에 없으면 = if you have only a little bit of time

시간이 전혀 없으면 = if you have no time at all

2.

내일 시간이 있으면 = if you have time tomorrow

오늘 시간이 있으면 = if you have time today

주말에 시간이 있으면 = if you have time on the weekend

다음 주에 시간이 있으면 = if you have time next week

이번 달에 시간이 있으면 = if you have time this month

3.

커피 마실래요? = Do you want to drink coffee? / Shall we drink coffee?

뭐 마실래요? = What do you want to drink? / What shall we drink?

어떤 거 마실래요? = What (kind of drink) do you want to drink?

어디에서 마실래요? = Where do you want to drink (something)?

4.

같이 커피 마실래요? = Do you want to drink coffee together?

저랑 커피 마실래요? = Do you want to drink coffee with me?

저랑 같이 커피 마실래요? = Do you want to drink coffee together with me?

다 같이 커피 마실래요? = Do you want to drink coffee with everyone?

Track 39

Sample Dialogue

Track
40

A: 어젯밤부터 지금까지 눈이 계속 오고 있어요.

B: 아마 길이 꽁꽁 얼 거예요. 조심하세요.

A: 네, 조심할게요.

A: *Since last night, it has been snowing non-stop.*

B: *The streets will probably be frozen. Be careful!*

A: *Okay, I will.*

Learn to Compare, Contrast, Modify,

✏ Exercises for Lesson *20*

Check the answers on **p.190**

Translate each phrase to Korean and write it in the space provided.

1. from last week until next week

( )

2. It is going to snow.

( )

3. I am going to study Korean.

( )

4. if you have no time at all

( )

5. Do you want to drink coffee with me?

(.)

BLOG

MOVIE THEATERS
(영화관)

Going to a 영화관 in Korea is not unlike going to a movie theater in any other country, but the experience of going to a Korean movie theater is what makes it unique. Most of the HUGE multiplexes like CGV, Lotte Cinema, and Megabox have state-of-the-art facilities with wide-screens and the ability to show 3D and 4D movies. There are even a few Lotte and CGV theaters in Seoul and Busan which offer 외국어 자막 (foreign subtitling)! However, if you are looking for a more intimate 영화관 setting, the smaller and independently owned 영화관들 have a bit of a "retro" feel since they do not have all the hype and bright lights of a gigantic multiplex.

How to purchase tickets

On the weekdays, you'll be able to purchase 영화 표 (movie tickets) by standing in line at the ticket booth (if the theater has one) or by using one of the automatic ticket machines. You can also use the online 예매 (reservation) system or a cell phone application to reserve your tickets and seats, which is the most convenient way to make sure you and your friends will have tickets!

It is HIGHLY recommended to purchase your tickets in advance using the theater's online reservation system if you are going to see a movie on 금요일 (Friday) or 토요일 (Saturday) nights, or even during holidays. Crowds are HUGE during these times, and more than likely, your show will be sold out if you wait until the last minute to get tickets.

To use the online reservation system, visit one of the websites listed at the end of this blog to purchase your tickets at the theater of your choosing. You can also use one of the automated ticket machines, but do not always assume there will be open seats! If you are going to a smaller theater, you may be able to get away with purchasing tickets from a ticket booth or the ticket machines on the day of the showing.

One thing you may want to note is that, for foreigners, there might be some difficulties when using the online reservation system or a mobile application. Sometimes they might ask for your 주민등록번호 (resident registration number). If you should run across this problem, you can visit CineinKorea.com to purchase tickets in English without having to use 주민등록번호, or ask your Korean friend to let you use his/her resident registration number, or simply go to the theater and buy your tickets there.

Ticket prices (March 2016)

Tickets are anywhere between 5,000W and 18,000W and depend on a variety of factors. Multiplexes in Korea have recently decided to subdivide the 가격 (price) of movie tickets. In the not too distant past, prices for a movie on a weekday were a bit lower than if you were to see the same movie on a weekend. Now, however, theaters have divided weekday movies into six different "time zones" (cheaper prices in the morning, more expensive prices at night) while weekends have been divided into three "time zones". The seating has also been divided into three seating zones: economy, standard, and prime. This division is quite similar to the way airline tickets are divided by price. Seats in "economy" are 1,000W cheaper than seats in the "standard" zone, while seats in the "prime" area are 1,000W more than the "standard" zone seats. Additionally, the type of movie you are seeing (regular 2D, 3D, 4D, IMAX) will also affect the price.

This price change with the subdivision of seats and times is incredibly new, and many people are unhappy about the change. There are even a few civil groups that have gone public about their displeasure with the new policy. It is unclear as to how long this new ticketing policy will remain in effect, but regardless of the recent changes, a 2D movie on a weekend is, on average, about 10,000W.

Cinema Websites (and other helpful stuff!)

If you choose to book your tickets on one of the following websites, you can choose almost any theater throughout Korea:

cineinkorean.com - English only
movie.interpark.com - Korean only
megabox.co.kr/booking - Korean only
cgv.co.kr/ticket - Korean only
lottecinema.co.kr/NLCHS/Ticketing - Korean only

You can use the following websites to book tickets for movies playing at that specific theater:

www.cgv.co.kr
www.megabox.co.kr
www.lottecinema.co.kr

If you want to download cell phone applications to reserve tickets, search "CGV 영화예매", "맥스무비 영화예매", "롯데시네마 모바일 APP", "인터파크 영화", or any other theater in your phone's marketplace or app store.

You can also dial "1330" from any phone (if you are using a cell phone, dial your area code first!) to find out showtimes, locations of movies, and instructions on how to get to the cinema in English. The Korea Tourism Organization (KTO) hotline operates 24 hours a day, 7 days a week and is a REALLY useful service for foreigners! If you are not sure about your area code, visit this website to find it: *http://www.visitkorea.or.kr/enu/GK/GK_EN_2_7_1.jsp*

Only 10 more lessons to go
until you are finished with Level 4!
Yay!

LESSON 21

Spacing in Korean

띄어쓰기 (Part 2)

Track 41

In Level 4 Lesson 16, you looked at the basic spacing rules when it comes to writing in Korean. You learned that independent words are written separately with a space between them, but there is no space between a noun, or a pronoun, and a marker. You also learned that certain words are used together so often that they are used and considered as just one independent word. In this lesson, you will learn more words that, over time, formed new meanings and are now being used as independent words. These words generally have different meanings from the combination of the original meanings of the combined words.

1. 돌려 주다 vs. 돌려주다

돌리다

= to turn; to revolve

돌려 주다

= to turn something for someone

돌려주다

= to return something; to give something back

Learn to Compare, Contrast, Modify,

2. 돌아 가다 vs. 돌아가다

돌다

= to turn; to turn around

돌아 가다

= to detour; to go around the long way

돌아가다

= to return; to go back to some place

3. 빌려 주다 vs. 빌려주다

빌리다

= to borrow

빌려 주다

= to borrow something (from someone else) for someone

빌려주다

= to lend something to someone

Track 41

4. 알아보다

알다

= to know

보다

= to see

알아보다

= to recognize something/someone; to look into something

알아 보다 does not exist.

129

5. 나오다/나가다

나다

= to be born; to get out; to be out of (not commonly used on its own)

오다

= to come

가다

= to go

나오다

= to come outside

　　*나 *does not have much meaning on its own; therefore, a space between* 나 *and* 오다 *is
not possible.*

나가다

= to go outside

6. 들어오다/들어가다

들다

= to get in; to be in; to get into (not commonly used on its own)

오다

= to come

가다

= to go

들어오다

= to come inside

들어가다

= to go inside

Sample Sentences

열쇠 돌려주세요.

= Please give me back the key.

언제 돌아갈 거예요?

= When will you go back?

돈 좀 빌려줄 수 있어요?

= Can you lend me some money?

한눈에 알아봤어요.

= I recognized it at once.

나가!

= Get out of here!

Track 41

들어오세요.

= Please come inside.

and Describe More Fluently in Korean!

Sample Dialogue

A: 현우 씨는 길거리에서 사람들이 많이 알아봐요?

B: 아니요. 그런데 제 목소리를 들으면 생각보다 많이 알아봐요.

A: 진짜요? 재미있네요.

A: *Hyunwoo, do many people recognize you on the street?*

B: *No, but more people recognize me than I expected if they hear my voice.*

A: *Really? Interesting.*

132

✎ Exercises for Lesson 21

Match each Korean word to its definition:

1. to turn something for someone

2. to come outside

3. to detour; to go around in a longer path

4. to recognize something/someone;
to look into something

5. to lend something to someone

a. 빌려주다

b. 돌아가다

c. 돌려주다

d. 나오다

e. 돌려 주다

f. 빌려 주다

g. 나 오다

h. 알아보다

i. 돌아 가다

Check the answers on **p.190**

133

LESSON **22**

Word Builder 5

장(場)

Track 43

The word element **장** is written as **場** in Hanja, and is fundamentally translated to English as "yard", "place", or "location". Now you can jump right into this lesson and start building some new words!

Sample Expressions

장 (yard/garden) + 소 (spot) = 장소 場所 = place; venue

> **Ex)**
> 시간, 날짜, 장소
> = time, date, place

운동 (exercise) + 장 (yard) = 운동장 運動場 = schoolyard; playground

> **Ex)**
> 어렸을 때 운동장에 나가는 거 굉장히 싫어했어요.
> = As a child, I really hated going out to the schoolyard.

134

주 (to stay) + 차 (car) + 장 (place) = 주차장 駐車場 = parking lot

Ex)

주차장에 주차하세요.

= Please park (your car) in the parking lot.

장 (place) + 면 (aspect/surface) = 장면 場面 = scene

Ex)

이 영화에서 제일 좋아하는 장면이 뭐예요?

= What is your favorite scene from this movie?

시 (city) + 장 (place) = 시장 市場 = marketplace

Track 43

Ex)

지금 시장 갈 거예요.

= I am going to the marketplace now.

목 (to grow) + 장 (yard) = 목장 牧場 = farm; ranch

Ex)

목장에서 갓 짠 우유 마셔 봤어요?

= Have you ever had milk straight from a cow on the farm?

수영 (swimming) + 장 (place) = 수영장 水泳場 = swimming pool = 풀장

Ex)

수영장에 일주일에 세 번 가요.

= I go to the swimming pool three times a week.

and Describe More Fluently in Korean!

예 (courtesy, etiquette) + 식 (ritual) + 장 (place) = 예식장 禮式場 = wedding hall

Ex)

예식장이 어디예요?

= Where is the wedding hall?

Alright! You have only learned everyday vocabulary until this point. Now, take a giant leap and take a look at some more academic words by learning a couple of scientific terms!

* 자 (magnetic) + 기 (energy) + 장 (field) = 자기장 磁氣場 = magnetic field

* 중 (heavy) + 력 (force) + 장 (field) = 중력장 重力場 = gravity field

Track 43

Learn to Compare, Contrast, Modify,

Sample Dialogue

Track 44

A: 수영할 줄 알아요?

B: 네. 그런데 수영장에서는 잘하는데, 바다에서는 못해요.

A: 왜요?

B: 무서워서요.

A: Do you know how to swim?

B: Yes. I swim well in the swimming pool, but I can't in the ocean.

A: Why not?

B: Because I'm scared.

137

✏ *Exercises for Lesson* **22**

Fill in the blanks with the appropriate Sino-Korean word.

1. The word element (   ) is related to "yard", "place", or "location".

2. Swimming pool

(   )

3. Marketplace

(   )

4. Wedding hall

(   )

5. Parking lot

(   )

Check the answers on **p.190**

Learn to Compare, Contrast, Modify,

LESSON 23

Word Contractions

축약형 (Part 2)

Track 45

In Level 4 Lesson 17, you learned one aspect of common word contractions in Korean: how the subject markers are contracted to shorter forms and attached to the previous words.

Ex)
저는 → 전
이것은 → 이건

Now that you see it, you remember, right? Perfect! Now you are ready to learn more word contractions in Korean!

First off, do you remember how to say "this", "that", and "it" in Korean?
For "this/the/that + noun", the words 이, 그, and 저 are used respectively.

이 책 = this book
그 가방 = the/that bag
저 자동차 = that car over there

139

When "this/it/that" are used as pronouns, the words 이것, 그것, and 저것 are used. The following are some expressions related to these words:

이렇다 = to be like this; to be this way

그렇다 = to be like that; to be that way

저렇다 = to be like that (over there); to be that way (over there)

If you want to use these as adverbs and say "like this", "in this way", or "in that way", use:

이렇게 = like this, in this way

그렇게 = like that, in such a way

저렇게 = like that (over there)

Track
45

Do you remember how to say "if" in Korean? It is "verb + -(으)면". If you want to review, go back to Level 2 Lesson 23, Level 3 Lesson 15, or Level 4 Lesson 1.

So, how do you say "if you do it like this" in Korean?

이렇게 하면 = if you do it like this

그렇게 하면 = if you do it in such a way

저렇게 하면 = if you do it like that

When combining "이렇다" (to be like this) with -(으)면 (if) to say "if it is like this", it creates 이러면 (the consonant ㅎ is dropped).

Learn to Compare, Contrast, Modify,

이렇다면 → 이러면
그렇다면 → 그러면
저렇다면 → 저러면

However, even when saying things such as "if you do it like this" using the verb 하다, it is also contracted to the same form.

이렇게 하면 → 이러면
그렇게 하면 → 그러면
저렇게 하면 → 저러면

Now you are ready to move on to something that is similar, but different in meaning. Do you remember how to say "how" in Korean? (We introduced this in Level 1 Lesson 24.)

Track 45

어떻게

When 어떻게 is combined with the 하다 verb, a contraction happens that is similar to the previous structure.

어떻게 하다 → 어떡하다 (more common in spoken Korean)

Ex)
(1) 어떻게 해요?

   = 어떡해요?

   = What are we supposed to do?

   = How should we deal with this?

141

(2) 어떻게 할 거예요?

    = 어떡할 거예요?

    = What are you going to do?

    = How are you going to take care of this?

어떡할 거예요? can be contracted even further into 어쩔 거예요?

Ex)

(1) 이거 어떡할 거예요?

    = 이거 어쩔 거예요?

    = How are you going to take care of this?

    = What are you going to do about this?

Track 45

(2) 이제 어떡할 거예요?

    = 이제 어쩔 거예요?

    = Now what?

    = How are you going to take care of it now?

Sample Dialogue

Track
46

A: 기계를 그렇게 발로 차면 어떡해요?

B: 고장 났어요.

A: 그래도요.

A: *How could you kick the machine like that?*

B: *It's broken.*

A: *Even so.*

143

Contract each phrase into something much shorter and much easier to say:

1. 그렇게 하면 (= if you do it in such a way)

→

2. 이렇다면 (= if it is like this)

→

3. 어떻게 해요? (= How should we deal with this?)

→

4. 어떻게 할 거예요? (= How are you going to take care of this?)

→

5. 어떻게 하지요? (= What do I do?)

→

Learn to Compare, Contrast, Modify,

LESSON **24**

Much (more), Much (less)

훨씬

In Level 2 Lesson 21 and Level 2 Lesson 29, you learned how to say "more", and also how to say that something is "more + adjective + than something". In this lesson, you will learn how to say "much more/less + adjective + than something".

Track 47

Although the Korean word for "much" (adverb) is 많이, in this case, a different word is needed: 훨씬.

Meaning

훨씬 = much (more), far (more), etc.

> **Ex)**
> 멋있다 = to be cool; to be stylish
> 더 멋있다 = to be cooler; to be more stylish
> 훨씬 더 멋있다 = to be much cooler; to be much more stylish

145

Sample Sentences

이게 훨씬 더 좋아요.

= This is much better.

서울에서 도쿄까지보다, 서울에서 뉴욕까지가 훨씬 더 멀어요.

= From Seoul to New York is much farther away than from Seoul to Tokyo.

일본어보다 한국어가 훨씬 더 쉬워요.

= 한국어가 일본어보다 훨씬 더 쉬워요.

= Korean is much easier than Japanese.

Track 47

훨씬 is the "much" in the phrase "much more", but when using 훨씬, people will already know that you are making a comparison; therefore, sometimes when you want to say "much more + adjective/adverb", the word 더 can be dropped from 훨씬 더.

* However, you cannot drop 덜 from 훨씬 덜, which means "much less + adjective/adverb".

Ex)

훨씬 더 좋아요. = 훨씬 좋아요.

훨씬 더 재미있어요. = 훨씬 재미있어요.

Examples of using 훨씬 with 덜.

* Go back to Level 4 Lesson 19 if you want to review 덜.

덜 = less

비싸다 = to be expensive

덜 비싸다 = to be less expensive

훨씬 덜 비싸다 = to be much less expensive

가깝다 = to be near

덜 가깝다 = to be less near

훨씬 덜 가깝다 = to be much less near

Track 47

147

Sample Dialogue

A: 이렇게 추운데 물에 들어갔
어요?

B: 물이 생각보다 훨씬 따뜻해요.

A: 그래요?

A: Did you go into the water even though it is
this cold?

B: The water is much warmer than you think.

A: Is it?

Learn to Compare, Contrast, Modify,

🖊 Exercises for Lesson 24

Translate each phrase to Korean:

1. to be much less expensive
   * 비싸다 = to be expensive

   (   )

2. to be much cooler; to be much more stylish
   * 멋있다 = to be cool

   (   )

Write each phrase in Korean on the lines provided below:

Check the answers on **p.191**

3. This is much better.

   ....

4. The traffic is much more inconvenient.

   ....

5. This is much less complicated.
   * complicated = 복잡하다

   ....

LESSON 25

-(으)ㄹ + noun (future tense noun group)

-(으)ㄹ + 명사, -(으)ㄹ 것

Track 49

There has never been a better time to start learning how to create and use future tense noun groups than right now!

verb stem + -(으)ㄹ + noun

The usages of this verb ending can be best explained through examples, but fundamentally, "verb stem + -(으)ㄹ" expresses the adjective form of a verb in the future tense.

Ex)

(1) 읽다 = to read → 읽 + -(으)ㄹ = 읽을
   → 읽을 책 = a book which (someone) will read; a book to read

(2) 초대하다 = to invite → 초대하 + -(으)ㄹ = 초대할
   → 초대할 사람 = a person who (someone) will invite; a person to invite

150

(3) 보내다 = to send → 보내 + -(으)ㄹ = 보낼

    → 보낼 편지 = a letter that (someone) will send, a letter to send

All of the examples above were in the "verb stem + -(으)ㄹ + noun" form.

When the word 것 (which means "thing" or "the fact") is used rather than a specific noun, the noun group can mean "something to + verb".

Ex)

(1) 먹다 = to eat → 먹 + -(으)ㄹ = 먹을

    → 먹을 것 = something to eat = food

    * 먹을 것 directly translates to "something to eat" or "thing(s) I will eat", but over the course of time, it has gained the meaning of "food".

Track 49

(2) 타다 = to ride → 타 + -(으)ㄹ = 탈

    → 탈 것 = something to ride = vehicle

    * 탈 것 directly translates to "something that I will ride" or "a thing that I will ride", but colloquially, it means "vehicle".

(3) 마시다 = to drink → 마시 + -(으)ㄹ = 마실

    → 마실 것 = something to drink = beverages

Now, do you recognize the ending -(으)ㄹ 거예요 from the lesson on future tense (Level 2 Lesson 1)? In future tense, add -(으)ㄹ 거예요 after a verb stem.

-(으)ㄹ 것 + 이에요 = -(으)ㄹ 것이에요 → -(으)ㄹ 거예요

151

Since the future tense stems from -(으)ㄹ 것, a Korean sentence like this can be translated in two different ways.

Ex) 이거 누가 먹을 거예요?

If you think of this sentence as "누가 먹다 (who + eat) + future tense", it will be translated as "who will eat this?" If you think of it as "누가 먹을 거 (who + will + eat + thing) + to be", it will be translated as "this thing, who will eat it?"

Sample Sentences

Track 49

내일 할 일이 많아요.

= I have a lot (of work) to do tomorrow.

= There is a lot of stuff that I will do tomorrow.

지금은 할 이야기가 없어요.

= Right now, I have nothing to say.

= For now, there is nothing I will say.

냉장고에 먹을 것이 전혀 없어요.

= In the refrigerator, there is not any food at all.

Learn to Compare, Contrast, Modify,

Sample Dialogue

Track 50

A: 뭐 먹을 거 없어요?

B: 주방에 한번 가 보세요.

A: 이거 먹어도 돼요?

B: 네, 드셔도 돼요.

A: *Is there anything to eat?*

B: *Go look around in the kitchen.*

A: *Can I eat this?*

B: *Yes, you can.*

153

Check the answers on **p.191**

_🖉_ Exercises for Lesson _25_

Translate each phrase to Korean and write it on the lines provided below:

_I._ a book that (someone) will read; a book to read

....

2. something to eat; food

....

3. work to do; stuff that I will do

....

4. clothes to wear

....

5. money to buy clothes

....

Learn to Compare, Contrast, Modify,

LESSON 26

-(으)ㄴ + noun (past tense noun group)

-(으)ㄴ + 명사, -(으)ㄴ 것

If you are studying these lessons in order, you just learned about "future tense noun groups" in the previous lesson. So, what better way to continue your studies than to now learn about past tense noun groups!

Track 51

$$\text{verb stem} + \text{-(으)ㄴ} + \text{noun}$$

The noun in this structure can either be the subject or the object of the verb. Thus, it is really important that you understand the context to figure out which one it is, but basically it means "something that someone did...".

Examples

1. 보다 = to watch; to see → 보 + -(으)ㄴ = 본
   → 어제 본 영화 = the movie that I saw yesterday

2. 오다 = to come → 오 + -(으)ㄴ = 온
   → 어제 온 사람들 = the people who came yesterday

155

3. 말하다 = to say; to talk about → 말하 + -(으)ㄴ = 말한

→ 친구가 말한 카페 = the cafe that a friend talked about

Sample Sentences

어제 본 영화 어땠어요?

= How was the movie that you saw yesterday?

새로 이사 간 집은 어때요?

= How is your new house that you moved to?

오늘 배운 내용 복습하세요.

= Please review what you learned today.

Track 51

Now, take a moment to compare a few different tenses for noun groups using what you have already learned from previous lessons.

Examples

1. 보다 = to watch; to read; to see

Present tense noun group: 보는 + noun
Past tense noun group: 본 + noun
Future tense noun group: 볼 + noun

제가 보는 책이에요.

= It is a book that I am reading.

Learn to Compare, Contrast, Modify,

제가 본 책이에요.

= It is a book that I have read.

제가 볼 책이에요.

= It is a book that I will read.

2. 공부하다 = to study

Present tense noun group: 공부하는 + noun
Past tense noun group: 공부한 + noun
Future tense noun group: 공부할 + noun

요즘 공부하는 외국어예요.

= It is a foreign language that I am studying these days.

Track 51

어제 공부한 외국어예요.

= It is a foreign language that I studied yesterday.

내일 공부할 외국어예요.

= It is a foreign language that I will study tomorrow.

157

Sample Dialogue

Track 52

A: 석진 씨, 다친 무릎은 괜찮아요?

B: 네. 다 나았어요.

A: 그래도 무리하지 마세요.

A: *Seokjin, is your hurt knee okay?*

B: *Yes, it is fully healed.*

A: *Still, don't strain it.*

Learn to Compare, Contrast, Modify,

✎ Exercises for Lesson 26

Write each phrase in Korean on the lines provided below:

1. the house that (someone) moved to

....

2. the movie that (someone) saw yesterday

....

3. the cafe that a friend talked about

....

4. the people who came yesterday

....

5. the earrings that (someone) received as a gift

....

Check the answers on **p.191**

159

LESSON 27

I think that…

… 것 같다

Track 53

The Korean verb for "to think" is 생각하다, but it is not commonly used to say "I think that …" in Korean. This is mainly because many Korean people think that this is too direct to say it in such a way. Instead, it is preferred to say "I think that…" using the following expression:

… 것 + 같다

같다 on its own means "to be the same", but when it is used with other nouns, it means "it is like…".

Ex)
학생 같아요.
= You are like a student. / You look like a student.
저 사람 한국 사람 같아요.
= He looks like a Korean person. / He is like a Korean.

160

In order to say "I think that …", what you need to do is know how to say that "something seems like" in combination with a "sentence".

Do you remember how to make noun groups for various tenses?

Past tense: -(으)ㄴ 것
Present tense: -는 것
Future tense: -(으)ㄹ 것

After that, you just add 같다 in order to express "I think that…"

Past tense: -(으)ㄴ 것 같다
Present tense: -는 것 같다
Future tense: -(으)ㄹ 것 같다

Track 53

Ex)
하다 = to do

Past tense: 한 것 같다
Present tense: 하는 것 같다
Future tense: 할 것 같다

벌써 한 것 같아요.

= I think (someone) already did it.

지금 하는 것 같아요.

= I think (someone) does/is doing it now.

내일 할 것 같아요.

= I think (someone) will do it tomorrow.

Sample Sentences

내일 비 올 것 같아요.

= I think it will rain tomorrow.

이게 더 좋은 것 같아요.

= I think this is better.

이거 뭔인 것 같아요?

= What do you think this is?

누가 한 것 같아요?

= Who do you think did it?

Track 53

곧 도착할 것 같아요.

= I think I will arrive soon.

While making sentences and hearing other people speak, you may notice that there are other ways to express "I think" in Korean besides - 것 같다. These will be covered in future lessons, but until then, you can practice using - 것 같다!

Learn to Compare, Contrast, Modify,

Sample Dialogue

Track 54

A: 언니, 제가 어제 파운데이션을 샀는데, 너무 어두운 색을 산 것 같아요.

B: 그래? 내가 같이 가서 맞는 색으로 골라 줄까?

A: 네.

A: *Eonni*, I bought a foundation yesterday, but I think I bought one that's too dark.*

B: *Did you? Do you want me to come with you and choose the right color for you?*

A: *Yes.*

* *"Eonni" is the romanization of* 언니: *a kinship term used when a female addresses an older, close female friend.*

and Describe More Fluently in Korean!

✏ Exercises for Lesson 27

Check the answers on **p.191**

Decide if the statement is "true" or "false" and circle your answer.

1. The verb for "to think" is 생각하다 in Korean.

    a. True   b. False

2. 같다 on its own means "to be the same".

    a. True   b. False

3. Adding -(으)ㄴ 것 makes noun groups for the present tense.

    a. True   b. False

4. There is only one way to express "I think" in Korean.

    a. True   b. False

5. Korean people use the word 같다 to say "I think".

    a. True   b. False

Learn to Compare, Contrast, Modify,

LESSON **28**

To become + adjective

-아/어/여지다 (Part I)

In Korean, the most basic and common way to say "to become + adjective" is:

Track 55

-아/어/여지다

Since all Korean adjectives are found in the dictionary in the infinitive form (-다), in order to say "to become + adjective", you need to know the infinitive form of the adjective.

Ex)
예쁘다 = to be pretty
예쁘 + -어지다 = 예뻐지다 = to become pretty

작다 = to be small
작 + -아지다 = 작아지다 = to become small

이상하다 = to be strange
이상하 + -여지다 = 이상해지다 = to become strange

165

재미있다 = to be interesting, to be fun

재미있 + -어지다 = 재미있어지다 = to become interesting

If you want to say "to become + more + adjective" in Korean, add "더" before the adjective.

Ex)

더 예뻐지다

= to become prettier

더 작아지다

= to become smaller

더 이상해지다

= to become stranger

더 재미있어지다

= to become more interesting

Track 55

Sample Sentences

날씨가 따뜻해졌어요.

= The weather has become warm.

컴퓨터가 빨라졌어요.

= The computer has become fast.

한국어 공부가 재미있어졌어요.

= Studying Korean has become fun.

Learn to Compare, Contrast, Modify,

줄이 길어졌어요.

= The line has become long.

내일 다시 추워질 거예요.

= It will become cold again tomorrow.

Sample Dialogue

Track
56

A: 너무 더워요. 에어컨 켜 주세요.

B: 에어컨 아까 켰어요.

A: 근데 왜 이렇게 안 시원해요?

B: 여기가 너무 넓어서 빨리 안 시원해
지는 것 같아요.

A: It's too hot. Please turn on the air conditioner.

B: I turned it on a while ago.

A: Then, why is it not cool like this?

B: This place is too big, I think, so it doesn't cool off
quickly.

Learn to Compare, Contrast, Modify,

✏ Exercises for Lesson *28*

Write the following in Korean:

1. to become small

( )

2. to become fast

( )

3. to become stranger

( )

4. The weather has become warm.

( )

5. The line has become long.

( )

Check the answers on **p.191**

and Describe More Fluently in Korean!

LESSON **29**

To gradually get to do, To end up doing

-게 되다

Track 57

By using the Korean structure **-게 되다**, you can say things like "to gradually get to do", "to eventually find oneself doing", or "to end up doing".

In order to fully understand and use this structure confidently, let's first take a look at what -게 and 되다 mean separately:

-게 = in such a way that... / so that...

되다 = to become

Meanings of -게 + 되다

= things happen in a way in which someone gets to do something

= to get into a state where someone does something

> ### Conjugation
> Verb stem + -게 되다

170

Examples

(1) 하다 (= to do) + -게 되다 = 하게 되다

[present tense] 하게 돼요.
[past tense] 하게 됐어요.
[future tense] 하게 될 거예요.

(2) 알다 (= to know) + -게 되다 = 알게 되다

[present tense] 알게 돼요.
[past tense] 알게 됐어요.
[future tense] 알게 될 거예요.

Track 57

Usages of -게 되다

-게 되다 has various usages:

I.
When you want to express that a situation has changed or happened due to an external influence, usually when you did not want, expect, or intend to do something, but you ended up doing it.

경은 씨랑 같이 일하게 됐어요.
= I got to work with Kyeong-eun.

A: 경화 씨, 미국으로 이사 가요? = Are you moving to the U.S., Kyung-hwa?
B: 네, 그렇게 됐어요. = Yes, it so happens that I am.

171

If you would like to mention what the external influence is, you can use -아/어/여서.

남편이 미국 회사에 다녀서 그렇게 됐어요.

= It happened because my husband works at an American company.

2.

When you want to talk about a result that you intended, but in a humble way.

좋은 회사에 들어가게 됐어요.

= I ended up getting into a good company.

Track
57

This person must have intended to go into a good company and put in a lot of effort to achieve it. However, this person is saying it this way because they are shy to talk about the good news or they do not want to sound like they are bragging.

3.

when you want to say that you (or someone else) will eventually do something in the future whether or not you (or he/she) want(s) to.

그렇게 하게 될 거예요.

= You will eventually end up doing it that way.

오게 될 거예요.

= He will eventually come here.

By using -게 될 거예요, you express confidence about what is going to happen in the future.

Sample Sentences

내일 알게 될 거예요.

= You will find out tomorrow.

다 사게 됐어요.

= I ended up buying everything.

다시 학교에 다니게 됐어요.

= (Things have happened so that) now I am going back to school again.

어떻게 여기에 오게 됐어요?

= How did you get to come here?

만나게 되면 말해 주세요.

= If you get to meet him, tell me.

Track 57

173

Sample Dialogue

Track
58

A: 날씨가 너무 추워졌어요.

A: The weather got too cold.

B: 추우니까 집에만 있게 돼요.

B: Because it's cold, I get to stay at home all the time.

A: 맞아요. 운동도 잘 안 하게 돼요.

A: Right. I rarely get to exercise as well.

Learn to Compare, Contrast, Modify,

✏ Exercises for Lesson 29

Write the following sentences in Korean:

1. He/She will eventually come here.

( )

2. You will find out tomorrow.

( )

3. I ended up buying everything.

( )

4. You will eventually end up doing it that way.

( )

5. How did you get to work here?

( )

Check the answers on **p.191**

LESSON **30**

Sentence Building Drill 2

Sentence Building Drill 2

Track
59

For the final lesson of Level 4, put everything you have studied to use by building some sentences!

Key sentence (1)

열 명 초대했는데, 아무도 안 올 수도 있어요.

= I have invited 10 people, but it is possible that no one will come.

Key sentence (2)

오늘은 어제보다 훨씬 따뜻한 것 같아요.

= I think today is much warmer than yesterday.

Key sentence (3)

지금 카페에서 어제 산 책을 읽고 있어요.

= Right now I am in a cafe, reading a book that I bought yesterday.

Learn to Compare, Contrast, Modify,

Expansion & variation practice with key sentence (1)

Original sentence:

열 명 초대했는데, 아무도 안 올 수도 있어요.

1.

열 명 = ten people

한 명 = one person

두 명 = two people

세 명 = three people

2.

초대했는데 = I invited (someone) but

말했는데 = I said but / I told (someone) but

조심했는데 = I was careful but

열심히 공부했는데 = I studied hard but

Track 59

3.

아무도 안 올 거예요. = No one will come.

아무도 모를 거예요. = No one will know.

아무도 안 할 거예요. = No one will do it.

아무도 초대 안 할 거예요. = No one will be invited; I will invite no one.

4.

안 올 수도 있어요. = (Someone) might not come.

안 줄 수도 있어요. = (Someone) might not give (somebody else) something.

안 그럴 수도 있어요. = It might not be so; It might not be the case.

안 웃길 수도 있어요. = It might not be funny.

177

Expansion & variation practice with key sentence (2)

Original sentence:

오늘은 어제보다 훨씬 따뜻한 것 같아요.

1.

어제보다 = than yesterday; compared to yesterday

지난주보다 = than last week; compared to last week

지난달보다 = than last month; compared to last month

작년보다 = than last year; compared to last year

Track 59

2.

어제보다 훨씬 따뜻해요. = It is much warmer than yesterday.

이거보다 훨씬 좋아요. = It is much better than this one.

한국어보다 훨씬 어려워요. = It is much more difficult than the Korean language.

3.

훨씬 따뜻한 것 같아요. = I think it is much warmer.

훨씬 좋은 것 같아요. = I think it is much better.

훨씬 재미있는 것 같아요. = I think it is much more interesting/fun.

Expansion & variation practice with key sentence (3)

Original sentence:

지금 카페에서 어제 산 책을 읽고 있어요.

1.

지금 책을 읽고 있어요. = I am reading a book now.

지금 운동을 하고 있어요. = I am working out now.

지금 음악을 듣고 있어요. = I am listening to some music now.

2.

카페에서 책 읽고 있어요. = I am reading a book in a cafe.

한국에서 일하고 있어요. = I am working in Korea.

여기에서 뭐 하고 있어요? = What are you doing here?

3.

어제 산 책 = the book I bought yesterday

그제 산 책 = the book I bought the day before yesterday

이번 주에 만난 친구 = the friend that I met this week

작년에 찍은 사진 = the picture that I took last year

**Track
59**

and Describe More Fluently in Korean!

Sample Dialogue

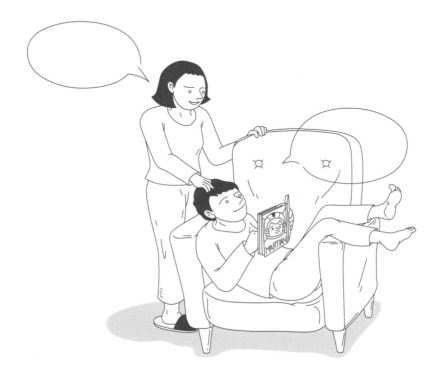

A: 왜 웃고 있어요?

B: 지금 읽고 있는 책이 너무 재미 있어서요.

A: 아, 이거 영화도 있지 않아요?

B: 네, 맞아요. 그런데 책이 훨씬 재 미있는 것 같아요.

A: Why are you smiling?

B: It is because the book that I am now reading is really entertaining.

A: Oh, isn't there a movie version as well?

B: Yes, there is, but I think the book is much better.

Learn to Compare, Contrast, Modify,

✎ Exercises for Lesson 30

Check the answers on **p.191**

Translate each phrase to Korean and write it on the lines provided below:

1. It might not be funny.

....

2. than last year; compared to last year

....

3. I think it is much more interesting/fun.

....

4. I am reading a book in a cafe.

....

5. the picture that I took last year

....

181

BLOG

Cheonggyecheon
(청계천)

서울 (Seoul) is much like any other major modern metropolis: a TON of traffic, people, and tall buildings. However, running right through the heart of the city is a little piece of nature called 청계천 (Cheonggyecheon). With 다리 (bridges), 징검다리 (stepping stones), and a gorgeous 폭포 (waterfall), this nearly-11 km (6.8 mile) body of water running from east to west has witnessed Seoul's transformation throughout its 600+ years as the capital of Korea.

In 1394, during the Joseon Dynasty, King 태조 (Taejo) decided to move the 수도 (capital) of Korea to 한양 (Hanyang), the former name of 서울 (Seoul). The capital city grew around the stream, separating the northern and southern parts of the city. Back then, 청계천 was known as "개천", which literally means "open stream" or "creek", and it eventually became part of 서울의 sewage system. The stream was fed by tributaries which flowed down from the surrounding mountains, and it was often bone-dry in the spring and fall, but frequently overflowed/flooded during the summer rainy season.

183

Today, 청계천 starts at 청계천 Plaza and stretches 8 kilometers (about 5 miles) to 살곶이공원 (Salgoji Park). 청계천 Plaza is roughly a 2,500 square meter area which was created based on the design of Korean traditional 보자기 (a colorful cloth used for wrapping) and features the elegant beauty of traditional stonework which is also very colorful, yet tasteful. At the plaza, there are always many events going on, from small open concerts to exhibitions. The closest subway station to this area is 광화문 (Gwang-hwa-mun) Station.

Renaissance of History and Culture (restoration)

The fountain at 청계천 was designed by Swedish sculptor Claes Oldenburg and is aptly titled "Spring". The 20-meter high sculpture was unveiled in 2005 and "...was designed to embrace the environment and nature by including water and light to feature the significance of the stream's restoration" (joongangdaily.com).

On steamy summer nights (or pretty much any other night) in Seoul, people gather at 청계천 to hang out and cool off. Coming to the stream is as much of a cultural activity as it is temporary relief from the sweltering heat of Seoul summers.

The waterfall is just one of the many great attractions of the restored 청계천 area. There is shopping nearby at 명동 (Myeongdong), as well as the Chinese Embassy, 광화문 (Gwanghwamun), Seoul City Hall, Kyobo Book Center, and many street food vendors!! If you find yourself hungry while visiting 청계천, fear not!! You can sanck on the street food to your heart's content!

During the colder months, the natural environment of the stream is accented by beautiful drawings by local artists, photos, musicians, and of course, the twinkling lights.

Whether you are taking a stroll along the water, viewing the stream from the street above, or sticking your feet into the crystal clear flow; you are experiencing an incredible amount of Korean history when visiting 청계천.

You have finished Level 4! 축하합니다*!!*

ANSWERS

for Level 4, Lessons 1 ~ 30

Answers for Level 4, Lesson 1

1. c

2. b

3. a

4. b

5. c

Answers for Level 4, Lesson 2

1. c

2. b

3. a

Answers for Level 4, Lesson 3

1. 모를 리가 없어요.

2. 안 추울 리가 없어요.

3. 안 아플 리가 없어요.

4. 갔을 리가 없어요

5. 내일 눈이 올 리가 없어요.

Answers for Level 4, Lesson 4

Level 4 Lesson 4

1. True

2. False - You use the -지(요) ending when both you and the other person know about something or have a common opinion about something, and you are just mentioning the fact again.

3. True

4. False - You can use the -지(요) ending as an interrogative (question) ending when you know about something, but you are asking yourself to confirm the fact. In this case, you do not speak in 존댓말.

5. False - You can use -지(요) when you do not know something, so you are asking yourself a question. Usually you are thinking out loud and asking the other people around you at the same time. 반말 is used in this case as well.

Answers for Level 4, Lesson 5

1. b. False

2. a. True

3. a. True

4. b. False

5. a. True

Answers for Level 4, Lesson 6

1. 동 (動)

2. 운동 (運動)

3. 작동 (作動)

4. 동물 (動物)

5. 동영상 (動映像)

Answers for Level 4, Lesson 7

1. 괜찮아요

2. 괜찮을 거예요

3. 괜찮았어요

4. 괜찮아요

Answers for Level 4, Lesson 8

1. 컴퓨터 켜도 돼요.

2. 내일 해도 돼요?

3. 이거 나중에 해도 돼요.

4. (그거) 안 먹어도 돼요.

5. (그거) 안 잘라도 돼요.

Answers for Level 4, Lesson 9

1. (그거) 열면 안 돼요.

2. (그거) 만지면 안 돼요?

3. 거기 들어가면 안 돼요.

4. 지금 말하면 안 돼요?

5. (그거) 던지면 안 돼요.

Answers for Level 4, Lesson 10

1. 사이에

2. 중에서

3. 사이에서

4. 사이에

5. 사이에서

Answers for Level 4, Lesson 11

1. 아무 데도

2. 아무나

3. 아무것도

4. 아무도

5. 아무거나

Answers for Level 4, Lesson 12

1. 이거 써 봤어요?

2. 들어가 볼까요?

3. 누구한테 물어볼까요?

4. 제가 알아볼게요.

5. 이거 해 보고 싶어요.

Answers for Level 4, Lesson 13

1. 부/불 (不)

2. 불만 (不滿)

3. 부정확 (不正確)

4. 부적절 (不適切)

5. 불편 (不便)

Answers for Level 4, Lesson 14

1. g

2. d

3. b

4. f

5. c

6. e

7. a

Answers for Level 4, Lesson 15

1. 아무렇게나

2. 아무것도

3. 아무 맛도

4. 아무한테도

5. 아무 말도

Answers for Level 4, Lesson 16

1. 부지런한 사람

2. 이거 샀어요.

3. 한국 여행

4. 한국관광공사

5. 빨리 말해요.

Answers for Level 4, Lesson 17

1. 이건

2. 넌

3. 어젠

4. 여긴

5. 그게

Answers for Level 4, Lesson 18

1a. 제일 and 가장

1b. 제일

2. 가장/제일 예쁜 여자

3. 가장/제일 좋은 것

4. 가장/제일 가까운 역이 어디예요?

Answers for Level 4, Lesson 19

1. 덜

2. 어제보다 덜 추워요.

3. 다, 다, 덜

4. 다, 덜

5. 덜

Answers for Level 4, Lesson 20

1. 지난 주부터 다음 주까지

2. 눈이 내릴 거예요 or 눈이 올 거예요

3. 한국어를 공부할 거예요

4. 시간이 전혀 없으면

5. 저랑 커피 마실래요?

Answers for Level 4, Lesson 21

1. e

2. d

3. i

4. h

5. a

Answers for Level 4, Lesson 22

1. 장 (場)

2. 수영장 (水泳場)

3. 시장 (市場)

4. 예식장 (禮式場)

5. 주차장 (駐車場)

Answers for Level 4, Lesson 23

1. 그러면

2. 이러면

3. 어떡해요?

4. 어떡할 거예요? or 어쩔 거예요?

5. 어떡하죠?

Answers for Level 4, Lesson 24

1. 훨씬 덜 비싸다

2. 훨씬 (더) 멋있다

3. 이게 훨씬 (더) 좋아요.

4. 교통이 훨씬 (더) 불편해요.

5. 이게 훨씬 덜 복잡해요.

Answers for Level 4, Lesson 25

1. 읽을 책

2. 먹을 것

3. 할 일

4. 입을 옷

5. 옷(을) 살 돈

Answers for Level 4, Lesson 26

1. 이사 간 집 or 이사한 집

2. 어제 본 영화

3. 친구가 말한 카페 or 친구가 이야기한 카페

4. 어제 온 사람들

5. 선물로 받은 귀고리

Answers for Level 4, Lesson 27

1. a. True

2. a. True

3. b. False (present tense ⇨ past tense)

4. b. False (only one way ⇨ many ways)

5. a. True

Answers for Level 4, Lesson 28

1. 작아지다

2. 빨라지다

3. 더 이상해지다

4. 날씨가 따뜻해졌어요.

5. 줄이 길어졌어요.

Answers for Level 4, Lesson 29

1. (결국 여기로) 오게 될 거예요.

2. 내일 알게 될 거예요.

3. 다 사게 됐어요.

4. (결국) 그렇게 하게 될 거예요.

5. 어떻게 여기서 일하게 됐어요? or 여기서 어떻게 일하게 됐어요?

Answers for Level 4, Lesson 30

1. 안 웃길 수도 있어요.

2. 작년보다

3. 훨씬 (더) 재미있는 것 같아요.

4. (저는) 카페에서 책(을) 읽고 있어요.

5. (제가) 작년에 찍은 사진

Notes On Using This Book

Colored Text
Colored text indicates that there is an accompanying audio file. You can download the MP3 audio files at **https://talktomeinkorean.com/audio**.

Hyphen
Some grammar points have a hyphen attached at the beginning, such as -이/가, -(으)ㄹ 거예요, -(으)려고 하다, and -은/는커녕. This means that the grammar point is dependent, so it needs to be attached to another word such as a noun, a verb, or a particle.

Parentheses
When a grammar point includes parentheses, such as -(으)ㄹ 거예요 or (이)랑, this means that the part in the parentheses can be omitted depending on the word it is attached to.

Slash
When a grammar point has a slash, such as -아/어/여서 or -은/는커녕, this means that only one of the syllables before or after the slash can be used at a time. In other words, -은/는커녕 is used as either -은커녕 or -는커녕, depending on the word it is attached to.

Descriptive Verb
In TTMIK lessons, adjectives in English are referred to as "descriptive verbs" because they can be conjugated as verbs depending on the tense.